From the Words of my Mouth

As a psychotherapist, in whose name do I speak? How can I come to speak in my own name? What does 'tradition' mean in psychotherapy? Originally published in 1993, the contributors to this book – all practising psychotherapists and teachers – explore these questions and investigate how theories and practices are passed on from one generation to the next. Their responses range over questions of training and indoctrination, the idea of tradition in the thought of Freud, Jung and Winnicott, and the implications of these questions for the practice of psychotherapy.

It will be of special interest to psychotherapists and counsellors, as well as students and teachers of therapy. With its emphasis on how psychotherapy might gain by seeing its connections to other traditions, such as literature, philosophy and the creative arts, the book will also appeal to a wider readership.

From the Words of my Mouth

Tradition in psychotherapy

Edited by

Laurence Spurling

Routledge
Taylor & Francis Group

LONDON AND NEW YORK

First published in 1993
by Routledge

This edition first published in 2014 by Routledge
27 Church Road, Hove BN3 2FA

and by Routledge
711 Third Avenue, New York, NY 10017

Routledge is an imprint of the Taylor & Francis Group, an informa business

A Library of Congress record exists under ISBN: 041506256X

ISBN: 978-1-138-01963-8 (hbk)
ISBN: 978-1-315-77881-5 (ebk)
ISBN: 978-1-138-01966-9 (pbk)

From the words of my mouth: tradition in psychotherapy

'Tradition' often conjures up ideas of conservatism and dogmatism, yet all that is radical, new or creative can only arise out of what has gone before. The contributors to this book, themselves practising therapists or teachers, are concerned to explore what the idea of tradition means in the practice of psychotherapy.

They investigate how knowledge, understanding and skills are passed from one generation to the next, asking themselves a number of questions: When I work with patients or teach students, in whose name do I speak? In the name of my own therapist, the people who trained me, or those who were 'first'? Is it in Freud's or Jung's name that I ultimately speak? In what way can I come to speak in my own name? The writers respond in a number of different ways – by wondering how a 'culture' of psychoanalytic thinking can be passed on from teachers to students; by considering how Freud's relationship to his Jewish heritage affected his creation of psychoanalysis; by examining the idea of tradition in the thought of Freud, Jung and Winnicott; by arguing that psychotherapy is best thought of as a version of 'scepticism'; and by reflecting on the violence done to both patients and to therapists when a tradition turns into a dogma.

From the Words of my Mouth will be of special interest to psychotherapists and counsellors, as well as students and teachers of therapy. With its emphasis on how psychotherapy might gain by seeing its connections to other traditions, such as literature, philosophy and the creative arts, the book will also appeal to a wider readership.

Laurence Spurling is a psychotherapist in private practice and Tutor on the Diploma in Adult Counselling Course, Birkbeck College, University of London. He is Assistant Director of the Squiggle Foundation, set up to cultivate the work of D. W. Winnicott.

From the words of my mouth: tradition in psychotherapy

Edited by Laurence Spurling

ROUTLEDGE

Tavistock/Routledge
London and New York

First published in 1993
by Routledge
11 New Fetter Lane, London EC4P 4EE

Simultaneously published in the USA and Canada
by Routledge
a division of Routledge, Chapman and Hall Inc.
29 West 35th Street, New York, NY 10001

Typeset in Baskerville by
Pat and Anne Murphy, Highcliffe-on-Sea, Dorset
Printed and bound in Great Britain by
Biddles Ltd, Guildford and King's Lynn

British Library Cataloguing in Publication Data
A catalogue record for this book is available from
the British Library.

Library of Congress Cataloging in Publication Data
From the words of my mouth: tradition in psychotherapy/
   edited by Laurence Spurling.
   p.   cm.
   Includes bibliographical references and index.
   1. Psychotherapy – Philosophy.   I. Spurling, Laurence, 1950–
   RC437.5.F75   1992   92–5063
   616.89'14'01–dc20   CIP

ISBN 0–415–06256–X
      0–415–06257–8 (pbk)

Contents

Contributors

David Aberbach is Associate Professor of Hebrew and Comparative Literature at McGill University, Montreal. He has written on literature and psychoanalysis for many journals, including *Commentary*, *Encounter*, *The Times Literary Supplement*, the *International Review of Psycho-Analysis* and *Moznayim*, and has published books on the Hebrew authors C. N. Bialik, Mendele Mocher Sefarim and S. J. Agnon, as well as a study of loss and literature, *Surviving Trauma: Loss, Literature and Psycho-analysis* (Yale University Press, 1989).

Nina Farhi's background is in politics and history. She now works in private practice and the National Health Service as a psychotherapist. She lectures on psychotherapy and is a member of the Training Committee of the Guild of Psychotherapists in London. She is the Director of the Squiggle Foundation which studies and cultivates the tradition of D. W. Winnicott.

Dr John Heaton is a psychotherapist in private practice. He is a founding member of the Guild of Psychotherapists, Chairman of the training committee of the Philadelphia Association (both in London) and Vice-President of the British Society for Phenomenology. He is the author of *The Eye: Phenomenology and Psychology of Function and Disorder*, and articles in scholarly publications.

David Hewison works as a psychiatric social worker, and is in private practice in London. He has lectured on Jung's life and work at City University, and is undertaking postgraduate work on Jung and Hermeneutics.

Zbigniew Kotowicz first qualified as a clinical psychologist and later trained as a psychotherapist. He held a private practice in London for several years, and is engaged in research in philosophy at the University of Warwick. His current work concentrates on the philosophical foundations of psychoanalysis and contemporary issues in Continental philosophy.

Ellen Noonan is Head of the Counselling Section at the University of London Centre for Extra-Mural Studies at Birkbeck College, where she has been designing and teaching courses since 1972. She trained as a clinical psychologist and psychotherapist at the Tavistock Clinic. Aside from teaching she has worked as a student counsellor and as a consultant specializing in organizational change and career development.

Laurence Spurling is a psychoanalytic psychotherapist in private practice in London, Assistant Director of the Squiggle Foundation, and a tutor at the Counselling Section at the University of London Centre for Extra-Mural Studies at Birkbeck College. He is the author of *Phenomenology and the Social World* (RKP 1977), editor of *Sigmund Freud: Critical Assessments* (Routledge 1989) and co-editor (with Ellen Noonan) of *The Making of a Counsellor* (Routledge 1992).

Introduction

Laurence Spurling

Hear, O sons, a father's instruction,
and be attentive, that you may gain insight;
    for I give you good precepts:
do not forsake my teaching.
    When I was a son with my father,
tender, the only one in the sight of my mother,
    he taught me, and said to me,
'Let your heart hold fast my words;
keep my commandments, and live;
    do not forget, and do not turn away
from the words of my mouth.'
    (Proverbs 4: 1–5, Revised Standard Version)

We just *can't* investigate everything, and for that reason we are
forced to rest content with assumption. If I want the door to turn,
the hinges must stay put.

                         (Wittgenstein, *On Certainty*)

'Tradition', warns Raymond Williams in his enquiry into the
'keywords' of modern thought, 'in its most general modern sense is a
particularly difficult word' (1976: 318). This difficulty is to do with
its uneasily ambivalent connotations. It is derived (and we will have
to note in passing the irony that in describing the meaning of the
term 'tradition' by investigating its derivations, we are ourselves
being traditional in seeking inspiration from the past) from the Latin
tradere, meaning to hand over or deliver. 'Tradition' denotes the
handing over of knowledge, or passing over a doctrine. It thus refers
to that which connects us to our parents and ancestors, and, by
extension, to the past in general as that which has brought into being
the culture and society in which we live. In this sense the word

conjures up ideas of necessary respect and duty. There is another meaning of *tradere*, which is to betray, to become a 'traitor' (this meaning is not found in the Hebrew word for 'tradition', *masorah*, which simply means the transmission of texts from one generation to another).

In its more modern usage 'tradition' – or, more usually, the adjective 'traditional' – has come to denote 'old-fashioned', an attitude of unthinking attachment to the past, and hence as an obstacle to change and innovation. The 'difficulty' of the word is thus a consequence of its ambivalent usage. On the one hand, it is the continuity without which there can be no change, it represents that which is fixed without which there can be no movement, the hinge which allows us to open the door, in Wittgenstein's image; on the other hand, it is that which stands in the way of our making progress, and which therefore has to be circumvented if not torn down.

These two poles – of that which allows change and that which prevents it – between which the word 'tradition' runs, can be illustrated by two images. The first comes from a description by the neurologist Oliver Sacks of a man suffering from Korsakov's psychosis. This man, called Jimmie, had suffered a catastrophic loss of memory such that the last thirty years of his life had become wiped out, so that his 'present' consisted of a bewildering world which was long dead. Although he could remember with clarity events of his childhood, he had no more than faint reminiscences of happenings since his memory came to a stop, and a memory span of contemporary events of no more than a few minutes, and sometimes only a few seconds. Consequently he was constantly misidentifying people around him, whom he confused with people of more than thirty years ago. When, in an attempt to inject a modicum of continuity into his life, Dr Sacks suggested to Jimmie that he keep a diary, and each day jot down notes of his thoughts and experiences, Jimmie kept losing the diary, so that it had to be attached to him. He then dutifully kept a brief daily notebook but could not recognize his earlier entries. The attempt failed, and Sacks writes of himself and his staff, 'none of us had ever encountered, even imagined, such a power of amnesia, the possibility of a pit into which everything, every experience, every event, would fathomlessly drop, a bottomless memory-hole that would engulf the whole world' (Sacks 1986: 34–5).

One tended to speak of him, instinctively, as a spiritual casualty – a 'lost soul': was it possible that he had really been 'de-souled' by a disease? 'Do you think he *has* a soul?' I once asked the Sisters. They were outraged by my question, but could see why I asked it. 'Watch Jimmie in chapel', they said, 'and judge for yourself'.

I did, and I was moved, profoundly moved and impressed, because I saw here an intensity and steadiness of attention and concentration that I had never seen before in him or conceived him capable of. I watched him kneel and take the Sacrament on his tongue, and could not doubt the fullness and totality of Communion, the perfect alignment of his spirit with the spirit of the Mass . . . There was no forgetting, no Korsakov's then, nor did it seem possible or imaginable that there should be; for he was no longer at the mercy of a faulty and fallible mechanism – that of meaningless sequences and memory traces – but was absorbed in an act, an act of his whole being, which carried feeling and meaning in an organic community and unity, a continuity and unity so seamless that it could not permit any break.

(1986: 36)

For this man, who seemed to have lost his very self in his inability to weave his experiences together into a meaningful fabric, the act of taking Communion put him back together again, by inserting him into a larger whole. In losing himself in a living and organic tradition, he was able to find himself. This is reminiscent of T. S. Eliot's contention, in his classic essay 'Tradition and the individual talent', that all creative art involves the appropriation by the individual artist of his artistic heritage, by which he situates himself in relation to those who have gone before. The artist must acquire what Eliot calls an 'historical sense', which means a form of 'self-sacrifice', an 'extinction of the personality' as the artist continually surrenders himself 'to something which is more valuable' (1973: 2016). Not only art but life itself needs a connection to something which grounds it, as the father in Proverbs reminds his sons.

But what if the words from our father's mouth tell us to see something that isn't there? This is what happens in the Hans Andersen tale, 'The emperor's new clothes', which gives us a very different image of tradition. In this story a fashion-loving emperor is tricked by two rogues who claim to be making a magnificent new garment for him out of cloth which has magical properties: even when made into clothes it is invisible to anyone who is either unfit for their job or very stupid. The emperor and his courtiers, under the spell of their fear of not believing, as well as their wish to believe, disregard the evidence of their own senses and are swept along by the charade. News of the wonderful garment spreads far and wide, and a large crowd gathers to watch the emperor when he first wears his new clothes in a royal procession. Everybody cheers and applauds, 'for nobody dared to admit that he couldn't see any clothes; this would have meant he was a fool or no good at his job'. The story ends thus:

> Then a child's puzzled voice was clearly heard. 'He's got nothing on!' 'These innocents! What ridiculous things they say!' said the child's father. But the whisper passed through the crowd: 'That child there says that the Emperor has nothing on; the Emperor has nothing on!'
> And presently, everyone there was repeating, 'He's got nothing on!' At last, it seemed to the Emperor too that they must be right. But he thought to himself, 'I must not stop or it will spoil the procession'. So he marched on even more proudly than before, and the courtiers continued to carry a train that was not there at all.
>
> (Andersen 1981)

Wisdom is now seen to reside not with the father's authority that comes from age and experience but with the innocence of the child who refuses to put aside the evidence of his own senses. His father, the emperor and all the others allow their own judgement to be determined by their idea of what they ought to see. In this image the power of authority and tradition is seen to rest on prejudice and wish-fulfilment, which crumbles when the people are finally brought to trust in their own experience rather than put their faith in received ideas.

Freud invoked a somewhat similar idea when, in showing how much of our mental life is unconscious, as well as dominated by the complexes and residues of our infantile sexual life, he claimed to be 'disturbing the peace of the world' (Freud 1916: 285). By depicting psychoanalysis as heir to the revolutionary spirit of the Enlightenment, Freud established it as a thoroughly modern discipline. In its questioning of what had previously been taken for granted, all forms of traditional authority were open to interrogation, if not subversion. Freud claimed to have revealed the irrational basis of group phenomena and the infantile roots of religious belief. Psychoanalytic therapy is founded on Freud's conviction that 'the liberation of an individual, as he grows up, from the authority of his parents is one of the most necessary though one of the most painful results brought about by the course of his development' (Freud 1907: 237).

Thus psychotherapy seems to be infused with the spirit of modernity and to oppose itself to the dead weight of tradition. And yet, turn to any psychotherapeutic journal and see how frequently its contributors take pains to place themselves in a line of thinking or practice which goes back to a recognized figure in the analytic world, and often back to the founding figures of Freud or Jung. Much analytically inspired writing comes over as deeply traditional, with an overwhelming priority placed on a knowledge of and respect for what has gone before, somewhat reminiscent of the style of Talmudic scholarship, with its characteristic and repetitive appeals, 'as rabbi so-and-so said', or, more simply, 'as it is said'. The institution of the 'training analysis', in which each student is analysed by an established and experienced therapist, is a form of handing on the knowledge and authority accumulated in the previous generation of teachers.

'IN THE BEGINNING': TRADITION AND ORIGINALITY

To think of a practice or form of knowledge in terms of tradition is to think of it in a temporal dimension, as what passes from one genera-tion to the next, a perspective which at some point takes us back to the very first generation, the point of origin of the tradition. This may be marked by the life of a particular figure in history, or it may be beyond memory and thus assigned to some mythological period.

There is already some sort of paradox here, for to conceive of a tradition is to locate it at some real or supposed temporal point, as having begun. Yet to think of its beginning includes an awareness of a time before the tradition came into being, and thus of con-sisting of knowledge and practices other than those embodied and expressed in the tradition. In other words, to be 'in' a tradition and to ask about how it started means to be able to think 'outside' of the tradition, to see it in a historical context as having developed out of something else.

Perhaps because of this paradoxical demand on our thinking, the notion of the beginning of a tradition comes to be invested with a particular resonance. It tends to be thought of, by those who come after, as a kind of unprecedented, absolute, once-and-for-all event. Thus, for example, the Bible begins with an account of the genesis of the whole world: 'In the beginning God created the heaven and the earth'.

These words come from the Authorized Version of King James. But the New English Bible has a different opening: 'In the beginning of creation, when God made heaven and earth . . .'. The NEB rendering has a similar structure to another translation by an Old Testament scholar.

> When God set about to create heaven and earth – the world being then a formless waste, with darkness over the sea and only an awesome wind sweeping over the water – God said, 'Let there be light'. And there was light.
>
> (see Josipovici 1988: 53–4)

This translation brings out more sharply what is already implied in the NEB translation where, by making the phrase 'in the beginning' dependent rather than independent, it is implied that there was already something *before* God created the world, unlike the traditional version, in which 'in the beginning' is an independent clause, which makes clear that everything began with God creating heaven and earth.

So when is a beginning not a beginning? It seems we are already lost in the intricacies of language and the ambiguities of translation. This has provoked one Bible scholar to note that our conception of God 'appears to be determined by grammar: only if his action enjoys the status of an independent sentence, and is therefore orginative, is he unlimited; if, on the other hand, creation is a dependent clause, then God too is subordinate to necessity' (quoted by Josipovici 1988: 58).

In this sense what comes first is determined by who comes after, and in particular how those who follow read or interpret the historical record. This is most evident when an oral tradition changes into a written one, a process marked by the establishment, in one form or another, of a canon, a list of writings which both carry and demarcate the authority of that tradition. In this process – whereby a written tradition comes to be constituted in a way which cannot be added to or detracted from, but can only be modified by subsequent commentary and interpretation – a tradition comes to be named, thereby creating itself through founding its own language. This language then gives its speakers the privilege of seeing the world from their own perspective. Such a perspective can appear to others, who do not share the same tradition and language, as a distortion.

So in the case of the Bible, what to the Jews is known as the 'Hebrew Bible' has been renamed by Christians the 'Old Testament'. In so doing, they have given a wholly different meaning to something which, for the Jews, is seen as self-sufficient: the 'old' Testament is now there in order to prefigure the 'new', which completes the old and thereby gives it its final meaning. (And so in the Christian canon the order of books in the Hebrew Bible is changed, ending not with the book of Chronicles, with the Jews returning to Israel after the Babylonian exile, but with the prophet Malachi's vision of God about to send his messenger to a disobedient Israel.)

Nevertheless in appropriating or misappropriating its Jewish heritage, the Christian tradition cannot but be marked by its origins, to which it has had to find a response. Thus the idea that what comes first is determined by who comes after has to be supplemented by its opposite, for it can also be said that what comes after is determined by what comes first. Although we cannot help but see the past through the eyes of the present, and can only apprehend a traditional text or writing through our current reading or interpretation of it, so that in a sense we are always creating our own past, we are still placing ourselves in a line of traditional authority which, as having already come into being, is always beyond our reach. We can never go back to the beginning of tradition, its origin has to remain hidden from us, for we can only imagine the beginning as something which has already happened – in which case it is no longer a beginning. Somehow, in a way we can never grasp, that which grounds our practice or knowledge, which seems a necessary and indeed essential component of our ability to see what it is we are doing, was once, at the time of its first coming into being, only one of a multitude of ways of doing things or of thinking, without any intrinsic significance of its own. The literary critic Harold Bloom, writing about the author of Genesis, calls this the 'factuality' of tradition: 'a kind of brute factuality or contingency inheres however in every historical tradition, be it philosophy or religion, literature or psychoanalysis, though such factuality usually blinds later representatives of a tradition from seeing that it is indeed factuality that imprisons them' (Bloom 1982: xvii). Within a tradition all reading is belated: the text has already been set by someone else whom we can never know. 'If to begin is to be free, such freedom [in the author of Genesis] becomes the freedom to rule those who come later, and such freedom to rule is authority, in a textual sense' (Bloom, ibid.).

'FROM THE WORDS OF MY MOUTH': TRADITION AND AUTHORITY

In the transmission of knowledge and experience from one generation to the next, what comes from the older generation is invested with authority. The son listens to his father – Proverbs tends to view the transmission of knowledge from father to son, but does also admonish the son to 'reject not your mother's teaching' (1: 8) – as the author of the words which he struggles to understand (and 'to understand' implies having someone to stand under). The father justifies his authority over his son by reminding him that he too was once a son in relation to his own father, who instructed him in the same way as he, the father, is now instructing his son.

The father thus appeals to the authority of the past. His words are seen, if you like, to speak for themselves. But the need to preserve the authority of tradition can lead to a fear and hatred of those who are seen as wanting to change it, and thereby betray it. For instance, a few verses before the end of the last book of the Bible, The Revelation to John, we find this admonition:

> I warn every one who hears the words of the prophecy of this book: if any one adds to them, God will add to him the plagues described in this book, and if any one takes away from the words of the book of this prophecy, God will take away his share in the tree of life and in the holy city, which are described in this book.
>
> (Revelation 22: 18)

Such a declaration not only refuses to countenance the exigencies of commentary and interpretation, which are predicated upon the incompleteness and ambiguities of meaning, as we have seen with the very first words of the Bible, it is also blind to its own history. For the words of Revelation, which demand that they must not be altered in any way, are themselves based on a Christian tradition which entailed a revision of the pre-existing Jewish law. The first Christian martyr, Stephen, was stoned to death after being accused by the Jewish authorities of being about to 'alter the traditions that Moses handed down to us' (Acts 6: 14, *New Jerusalem Bible*). Jesus set the tone for this enquiry into the meaning or spirit of the Jewish law by declaring, 'The sabbath was made for man, not man for the sabbath' (Mark 3: 27).

This revolutionary-sounding statement by Jesus is an attack on an unthinking adherence to the letter of the law rather than taking account of its spirit. Interestingly, however, it is preceded by an appeal to precedent within the Jewish heritage itself, namely an occasion when David took food forbidden to those who were not priests in order to feed himself and his followers who were hungry (Mark 3: 23–6). Jesus thus turns the weapons of his accusers against them by also appealing to traditional authority, although for his own purposes. This appeal turns on the ambiguities of reading, interpretation and transmission which we have already noted.

In other words, the authoritative transmission of a tradition is never as monolithic as it might appear. When embodied in a text, this text is treated as being in need of preservation and protection. Yet its range of meanings, of allusions and implications, extends far beyond what may have been intended by its original authors, who can never control how future readers will understand or use what they have written. The elasticity of authority, to connect one generation to the next, is always liable to be overstretched. It may be this very indeterminacy in the nature of its authority that encourages traditions to spread, to enlarge their claims to explain whatever comes within their orbit (there is a connection between the Latin *augere*, to increase, via *auctus*, an auction, to *auctor*, an author, which is the root of *authority*). It is not easy to set the limit of that to which a tradition refers. At its extreme, a tradition may claim to be all-encompassing. In the *Mahabharata* the monk Utanka announces, 'whatever is found in this story may be found somewhere else; but nothing found anywhere else will not be found in this story' (quoted by McConnell 1986: 3).

PRESERVATION AND PURITY: TRADITION AND THE DEVELOPMENT OF PSYCHOANALYSIS

These remarks on the meaning and nature of tradition raise a host of questions and queries: for example, about what is to count as a tradition, about whether there are different kinds of traditions, some more open to change and revision than others, about how exactly traditions come into being, how they are transmitted and how they are kept alive and may grow.

With these questions in mind we can consider the field of psychotherapy and its most important modern development, psychoanalysis, in response or reaction to which most schools of psychotherapy have developed. Psychoanalysis, if it can be spoken of as a tradition, was a tradition founded by one man. At a certain point in his career, when he had formulated most of his fundamental ideas, Freud gathered round him a group of disciples and students, and became concerned with how psychoanalysis would be handed on. In *The Question of Lay Analysis* he mapped out his ideas of what he then, in 1926, called the 'fantastic idea' of a 'college of psychoanalysis'. Much would have to be taught, he writes, which would also be found in a medical faculty:

alongside of depth-psychology, which would always remain the principal subject, there would be an introduction to biology, as much as possible of the science of sexual life, and familiarity with the symptomatology of psychiatry.

He continues:

On the other hand, analytic instruction would include branches of knowledge which are remote from medicine and which the doctor does not come across in his practice: the history of civilization, mythology, the psychology of religion and the science of literature. Unless he is well at home in these subjects, an analyst can make nothing of a large amount of his material.

(Freud 1926: 246)

Freud here has a wide-ranging vision of the kind of knowledge the practising psychoanalyst needs to have, a knowledge drawing on a familiarity with history, mythology and literature. Freud often said that he had not discovered anything new, that it had all been said before by poets, novelists and dramatists. Here is the sense of psycho-analysis as heir to what has gone before, although this notion of 'what has gone before' has been widely dispersed over several different disciplines. Psychoanalysis as a form of knowledge in its own right would have to take its place among established traditions of knowledge and enquiry.

At the same time, while acknowledging how psychoanalysis gathers together what has gone before, the product of this process – what Freud calls 'depth-psychology' – is seen as something original in its own right. Depth-psychology would be the 'principal subject', the core around which ideas and insight from other sources and fields would be grouped. The relationship between the ideas of this princi-pal subject and those derived from the fields of literature, mythology, etc. is not here addressed. However on other occasions Freud has used the metaphor of purity, in speaking for instance of the need to preserve the 'pure gold' of psychoanalysis from the 'base metal' of other forms of psychotherapy (Freud 1919: 168). In such a way of thinking psychoanalysis is something which must be protected against contamination by what is both foreign and less pure.

Thus, as well as drawing on other sources of traditional knowledge, Freud envisages psychoanalysis, or at least its core, as itself consti-tuting a particular form of knowledge and practices which have to be handed on in as pure a form as possible. In this sense psychoanalysis comes to be constituted as a tradition in its own right. It is seen as a new departure from other areas of knowledge, marking a break with what has gone before.

To call psychoanalysis a tradition is, as we have seen, to draw attention to several features of how this knowledge is viewed. There is seen to be a core or kernel of ideas, practices, etc., which are held to constitute the essence of the tradition, which have to be passed on in as faithful a manner as possible. Freud, as the author of psychoanalysis, took it upon himself to authorize what could and could not count as proper or pure psychoanalysis. For instance in 1923, in an article explaining psychoanalysis for inclusion in a German encyclopaedia, he defined it as follows:

> *The Corner-Stones of Psycho-analytic Theory*: The assumption that there are unconscious mental processes, the recognition of the theory of resistance and repression, the appreciation of the importance of sexuality and of the Oedipus complex – these constitute the principal subject-matter of psycho-analysis and the foundations of its theory. No one who cannot accept them all should count himself a psycho-analyst.
>
> (Freud 1923: 247)

Here Freud lays down the cornerstones of psychoanalysis, which serve to distinguish what is to count as psychoanalysis from what is not. What Freud does here is analogous, in the world of business, to establishing a copyright or franchise for a particular product and, in the theological world, to marking out a dogma, to which all must profess allegiance.

In constituting itself as a tradition in its own right, psychoanalysis is seen as having made a decisive break with what went before, that it has inaugurated something decisively new. There is therefore a tendency, for those who profess to follow Freud, the originator of this tradition, to write about him as though he sprang from nowhere, and his achievements as though they are without precedent. For instance Erik Erikson, in an essay on Freud called 'The first psychoanalyst', refers to Freud's work on his own dreams in the period leading up to the publication of *The Interpretation of Dreams* as 'the first self-analysis in history' (Erikson 1964: 34). In this phrase the writer 'forgets' all other examples of biographical confessions and attempts at self-understanding which have gone before, and which perhaps culminated in the Romantic movement, in order to establish the absolute originality of what Freud did. From within a tradition, as we have seen, the history of that tradition comes to be written as though it arose *sui generis*.

Once a body of knowledge or practices come to be seen as a tradition, the originator or originators of this tradition are invested by those who follow them with a unique and binding form of knowledge or insight. Authorship becomes authority. This traditional authority can then legitimize the setting up of some form of method or organization for the passing on of the tradition, based on an appropriate form of personal relationship, such as that of master–disciple or teacher–pupil, in which students are initiated or apprenticed. This is what happened in psychoanalysis. A committee was set up to preserve the essence of its ideas, and formal training institutes were established to oversee the handing on of the tradition.

SPEAKING IN ONE'S OWN NAME

But, as we have indicated, the handing over of traditional knowledge and practices is not unproblematic. There is always a tension between what cannot be questioned and what can, between the authority and weight of the past and the uniqueness of the present. This issue is of particular importance in psychoanalysis for, like all forms of psychotherapy, it is dedicated to freeing the patient from all forms of oppressive and neurotic authority which prevent him from thinking and acting in his own right. But this aim of liberation from authority is achieved by the patient submitting – however this is actually understood – to the authority of the therapist or of the therapy, at least initially, for the process of therapy to get under way. If the aim of psychoanalysis is, in Bion's happy phrase, to introduce the patient to himself, this can only be done via the decisive intervention of the analyst.

On this view, which sees psychoanalysis as that which enables the patient to speak in his own right, it would seem to be a minimum requirement of the analyst that he himself should have acquired this capacity. This means that he must pay attention to where or how he locates himself in terms of his own tradition. One way of doing that, argued by François Roustang in his book *Dire Mastery: Discipleship from Freud to Lacan*, is to employ the methods of psychoanalysis on itself.

> In order to question analysis, one must first stop being fascinated by theory and analyze the fantasies or desires that gave rise to it; one must analyze theory as the text of a dream or myth.
>
> (Roustang 1982: 58)

Here Roustang argues for the adoption of a certain kind of perspective which will lessen, if not dissolve, the authority and factuality of a theory. Theory, he says, legislates and authorizes by laying down in advance how one should think. He claims that this runs counter to the spirit of psychoanalytic enquiry, in which one never knows in advance what a given phenomenon will mean. Meanings are only revealed in retrospect, in the light of events and fantasies which come later (expressed in Freud's idea of 'deferred action'). Thus the meaning of theory, what it says, cannot be known in advance, but only by a retrospective analysis of how it came about. The psychoanalyst thus has to retrace the steps leading to the birth of his own tradition, and think them through again for himself, which Roustang refers to as analysing the fantasies or desires which gave rise to psychoanalysis. In a certain sense, then, each analyst, in order to make the theory his own, has to know Freud better than Freud knew himself.

The key to this, according to Roustang, is no longer to be 'fascinated' by theory. This means, in psychoanalytic terms, that each analyst has to address his own transference to Freud and to psychoanalytic theory. Roustang's choice of the word 'fascination' is interesting, as the word derives from the Latin *fasces*, a bundle of authoritative rods, which has a direct link with 'fascism'. *Fasces* is probably linked to another Latin word, *fascinus*, 'which may originally have designated a magical operation in which one tied up the victim' (Partridge 1966: 201). Thus the word reminds us of the violence perpetrated by and on those who are spellbound by an authority. In psychoanalytic institutes and societies the fascination is most evident, according to Roustang, by the phenomenon of discipleship, in which the student can only speak in the name of his master (be it his teacher, analyst, or figure of authority such as Freud). Only when the student can free himself from this fascination, which ties him to the master, can he begin to speak in his own name, and thereby become worthy of being an analyst.

This liberation from the fascination of theory is, however, an activity of great tension and difficulty. It is, indeed, seen as on a par with the patient's attempt to free himself from his illness, as Roustang indicates by the language he uses: theory must be 'repressed' during the session (1982: 70), theory can function as a 'defence' or 'symptom', just as disciples for the master can serve as his *garde-fou*, his protection from the madness of solitary thought (p. 34). Thus, for Roustang, fascination with theory serves ultimately as a defence against psychosis.

In speaking of the fascination of theory and the power of dis-cipleship Roustang is drawing attention to precisely those issues of originality, transmission and authority which have been discussed as features of tradition. In psychoanalytic discourse it is 'theory' which has to be passed on, 'theory' being understood as a more-or-less coherent body of hypotheses, concepts and ideas which both inform and find expression in 'technique', a series of observations, admoni-tions and rules-of-thumb about practice. 'Theory', in this particular embracing usage, can then be seen as a way of expressing part of that which makes up the core or kernel of a tradition, and which must be preserved in the process of transmission, at a particular point in time; whereas 'tradition' moves diachronically rather than synchronically as it shifts one's attention to questions of history and origins.

From this temporal perspective we can give another twist to Roustang's warnings of the seductions of theory becoming used as a defence against madness: fascination with theory can also be seen as a defence against death. In the Book of Ecclesiasticus one of the benefits of fatherhood is described thus:

Even when the father dies, he might well not be dead,
since he leaves his likeness behind him.
In life he had the joy of his company,
dying, he has no anxieties.
He leaves an avenger against his enemies
and a rewarder of favours for his friends.

(30: 4–7, *New Jerusalem Bible*)

In this passage the family is celebrated as that which preserves the life of one generation in the generation to come. The relationship between father and son could be described as an example of what the philosopher Emmanuel Levinas calls 'filiation', in which the father sees his son not in terms of power or ownership but as representing his own potential but unrealized possibilities: 'the fact of seeing the possibilities of the other as your own possibilities, of being able to escape the closure of your identity and what is bestowed on you, toward something which is not bestowed on you and which neverthe-less is yours – this is paternity' (Levinas 1985: 70). This play between seeing the son as both 'mine' and as essentially 'other-than-me' has resonances with Winnicott's description of a healthy family as a group built up on loyalties, but which allows the growing child a con-tinuing 'experimentation with disloyalties' (1986: 138), both within and without the family group.

Winnicott also draws attention to the 'strain and stresses' of this process. 'The most aggressive and therefore the most dangerous words in the languages of the world are to be found in the assertion I AM' (1986: 141). It is this assertion – which calls to mind not only the demand for recognition of the child or disciple, but also the declaration of authority of the parent or master, the 'I am that I am' of the God of Exodus – or, rather, the fear of it being spoken, which seems to transform the recognition of 'family likeness' into a neurotic or even psychotic relationship of authoritarian master and submissive disciple.

This theme of the dangers of received theory, of how it can stifle creativity and destroy the spontaneity of the therapist, runs through the writings of some of the best psychoanalysts, perhaps most notably in some of the later works of Wilfred Bion. In a talk given in New York, in answer to a question about the value of psychoanalytic concepts and 'working hypotheses', Bion replied as follows:

I think they are quite useful for about three sessions – if you are lucky enough to see the patient on three successive occasions. You know nothing whatever about the patient and therefore have to formulate some sort of theoretical opinion – the theories in that instance taking the place of facts, because there are no facts. After that you hope not to allow your theoretical preoccupations to obscure the impressions to which you should be exposing yourself. This is not easy to do – there would be something seriously wrong with your patient if he couldn't make a fool of you. At the same time there is something seriously wrong with the analyst who cannot allow himself to be made a fool of; if you tolerate it, if you can tolerate being angry, then you may learn something. Never mind about all these theories of what analysis *ought* to be; what we ought to be is a matter of no importance in the *practice* of psychoanalysis or in the practice of any part of real life. It does matter what we are.

(Bion 1980: 38)

Both Roustang and Bion speak of 'theory' as that which guides the analyst, that which he brings to bear on what happens in a session in order to make some sense of it. Each, in his own way, spells out the dangers of reliance on theory, how the analyst needs to keep a critical distance from theory, indeed how theory has at times to be dispensed with. But if the analyst must 'forget' theory, 'repress' it in order to learn and to practise, on what does he draw when he is free from theory; on what ground does his particular skill and expertise rest? Bion's answer is that what matters is 'what we are'. But this phrase, which can come happily from the mouth of such an experienced and original analyst as Bion, lends itself too easily to misuse, for example as a buttress to being thoughtless, sentimental or narcissistic with one's patients.

Furthermore if theory is to be dispensed with, it must have first been acquired. Roustang acknowledges that psychoanalysis still needs to be transmitted and taught, otherwise it would cease to exist. There is an inescapable circularity here. What is taught then has to be forgotten in order for it to be properly learnt.

One conclusion drawn by Roustang from his discussion of disciple-ship is that because the transmission of theory inevitably fosters trans-ference, there are no good psychoanalytic societies (1982: 34). But perhaps the very notion of a 'good' psychoanalytic society – as well as a 'good' training, theory, technical procedure or, indeed, a 'good' therapist – needs to be reconsidered. Just as the patient is required to re-think the assumptions and categories that have informed his life so far, to put received or taken-for-granted ideas up against the growing capacity to think for himself, so is the therapist, fired by considera-tions of where his knowledge and skill come from and on what they might rest, led on to a path which might lead to all kinds of subversive, disquieting or exhilarating thoughts.

These introductory remarks can be seen as the frame within which the authors of the following chapters have been asked to work. Each has been asked to limit his or her conception of 'psychotherapy' to that of 'dynamic psychotherapy' or 'depth psychology', but no restriction has been placed on how the idea of tradition is to be understood. The chapters can be read as first attempts to explore the relationship between psychotherapy and tradition. They address the teaching of psychotherapy, whether transmission can be distinguished from indoctrination, and from which sources, historical and personal, therapists might draw inspiration which makes their work both possible and worthwhile. Some of these sources are literary, theologi-cal, alchemical, philosophical or what might be called everyday (for example the idea of 'playing'). There are inevitably gaps in such a list, perhaps most notably a consideration of the subject from a political and from a feminist perspective, but the book will have served its purpose if it can stimulate others to pursue the relationship between psychotherapy and tradition in their own way.

REFERENCES

The Revised Standard Version was the source for Bible quotations unless otherwise indicated.

Andersen, H. (1981) *Hans Andersen's Fairy Tales*, translated by N. Lewis, London: Penguin Books.
Bion, W. (1980) *Bion in New York and Sao Paulo*, edited by F. Bion, Perthshire: Clunie Press.
Bloom, H. (1982) Introduction to *On the Bible* by Martin Buber, New York: Schocken Books.
Eliot, T. S. (1973) 'Tradition and the individual talent', in *The Oxford Anthology of English Literature*, vol. II, edited by F. Kermode and J. Hollander, New York: Oxford University Press.
Erikson, E. (1964) *Insight and Responsibility*, London: Faber & Faber.
Freud, S. (1909) 'Family romances', in *Standard Edition of the Complete Psychological Works of Sigmund Freud*, 24 vols, 1953–74, edited by J. Strachey, London: Hogarth Press (SE) 9.
—— (1916) *Introductory Lectures on Psychoanalysis*, SE 16.
—— (1919) 'Lines of advance in psycho-analytic theory', in SE 17.
—— (1923) 'Two encyclopaedia articles', in SE 18.
—— (1926) 'The question of lay analysis', in SE 20.
Josipovici, G. (1988) *The Book of God*, New Haven, Conn.: Yale University Press.
Levinas, E. (1985) *Ethics and Infinity*, translated by R. Cohen, Pittsburgh, Pa.: Duquesne University Press.
McConnell, F. (1986) *The Bible and the Narrative Tradition*, New York: Oxford University Press.
Partridge, E. (1966) *Origins*, London: Routledge & Kegan Paul.
Roustang, F. (1982) *Dire Mastery: Discipleship from Freud to Lacan*, translated by N. Lukacher, Baltimore, Ma.: Johns Hopkins University Press.
Sacks, O. (1986) *The Man Who Mistook his Wife for a Hat*, London: Picador.
Williams, R. (1976) *Keywords*, London: Fontana Press.
Winnicott, D. (1986) *Home Is Where We Start From*, Harmondsworth: Penguin Books.

Chapter 1

Tradition in training

Ellen Noonan

INTRODUCTION

Courses in psychoanalytic counselling have been offered at the University of London Centre for Extra-Mural Studies for twenty years. During that time the provision has expanded from a single Certificate in Student Counselling to some fifteen courses, spanning the range from general access introductions to highly selective Diploma and Advanced courses. There are intermediate level courses for specific professional groups or settings. Although the courses vary a great deal in intensity, depth and demand, they share at least four underlying assumptions and aims.

The first is that learning is a total experience, calling on and changing both intellectual and emotional resources. Consequently the courses have strong theoretical components, giving students a solid theoretical framework for their work, while also creating opportunities for students to reflect on what these ideas mean to them in the context of their personal lives. Additionally, the courses emphasize the importance of emotional maturity as a professional requirement and provide regular groups for students to explore their personal and professional attitudes and feelings.

Second, the courses are meant to be immediately useful to the students in their work. They are designed as in-service trainings, so that students may continually apply and evaluate what they are learning, both by bringing material from work to the course for discussion and by taking knowledge and skills into the work place 'tomorrow'. There are case discussion groups and practical skills sessions to achieve this aim.

Third, an understanding of the organizational settings in which the students work is regarded as essential so that they may appreciate how the environment affects their work and how they may contribute to the good functioning of their organizations. Some courses have a residential group relations workshop to focus on these issues, but all courses study their own functioning as a learning institution.

Finally, and indeed informing all the other assumptions, psycho-analysis by virtue of the applicability of its intensive methods for understanding unconscious processes in individuals, groups, institu-tions and society, is deemed to provide a rich framework for learning about human behaviour, therapeutic skills and professional attitudes, all of which are relevant to counselling. All courses are based on psychoanalytic theory and are taught by analytically oriented analysts, psychotherapists and counsellors.

This chapter explores this last 'tenet' of the courses, drawing particularly on our experience of our Diploma courses. These meet for a day a week over two academic years, and include the residential workshop. They have a membership of twenty students, who are selected by individual and group interviews, during which particular attention is paid to their suitability for the course in terms of their potential to learn and use the concepts and to benefit from the methods of teaching. At the end of the course they are evaluated on their theoretical knowledge, counselling ability, and professional attitudes through a combination of academic and professional assess-ments. By looking at various elements of the courses' structure and methodology which are predicated on psychoanalytic ideas, this chapter aims to explore how the courses partake of and perpetuate the psychoanalytic tradition.

TEACHING AND THE PSYCHOANALYTIC TRADITION

Sensibilities about boundaries in the psychotherapeutic professions may feel somewhat bruised by the inclusion of this chapter because counselling is ostensibly so far from the pure gold of psychoanalysis. Freud himself worried about contamination of his fragile psycho-analysis, but he was also torn between the desire for purity and the wish for extension. In 'The question of lay analysis', Freud writes,

Our civilization imposes an almost intolerable pressure on us and it calls for a corrective. Is it too fantastic to expect that psycho-analysis in spite of its difficulties may be destined to the task of preparing mankind for such a corrective? Perhaps once again an American may hit on the idea of spending a little money to get the 'social workers' of his country trained analytically and to turn them into a band of helpers for combating the neuroses of civilization.

(Freud 1926: 250)

But, whatever form this psychotherapy for the people may take, whatever the elements out of which it is compounded, its most effective and most important ingredients will assuredly remain those borrowed from strict and untendentious psycho-analysis.

(Freud 1919: 168)

The ambiguity of the lines of distinctiveness between psychoanalysis, psychoanalytic therapy and psychoanalytic counselling is not easy to dispel. Attempts to draw the lines according to criteria about practice or about training do not always hold in the reality of the work, although they do have substance in the minds of the practitioners, particularly when it comes to aspects such as commitment, sacrifice and status. (It is noticeable, for instance, that counsellors will upgrade themselves to psychotherapists when referring to their work, but the reverse seldom occurs.) However, if psychoanalytic counselling accepts that it is number three in this hierarchy, it claims to be number one in the hierarchy of schools of counselling, that is, more powerful, more inclusive, more demanding than any of the schools which came into being as splinters from psychoanalysis: Person-centred, Transactional Analysis, Gestalt, Primal Scream, and so on. As we patrol and guard this boundary which separates psychoanalytic counselling from the 'new therapies' we are revealed to be deeply conservative, deeply traditional, deeply steeped in the culture of psychoanalysis, and much more desirous of establishing our blood relationship with psychoanalysis.

These border skirmishes can give rise to much discomfort and defensiveness, when it feels as if our identity and integrity are under attack. It is salutory to remember that the training which is being considered here is the outcome of an opportunity, a challenge, and ultimately an experiment. It represents an attempt to offer a training in the essential aspects of psychoanalytic theory and technique to people who are wanting to do something therapeutic amidst the complex forces of the 'market-place' (as opposed to the relative simplicity of the consulting room) and to design that training in the light of what psychoanalysis has to say about teaching and learning. This was immensely helped by the fact that the course was to be placed in a university and the first course was to be specifically for counsellors of students: we had to concentrate on the problems and processes involved in the learning role, learning institutions, and the student–teacher relationship in both the content and the structure of the course.

From the very outset in our thinking we borrowed from the literary tradition of seeking a form or structure which in and of itself would contribute to an understanding of the ideas being presented in the content of the course: we aimed for a structure which would enable students to 'learn as they learned', by demonstrating the ideas of psychoanalysis in the practice of the course. The meaning of this rather clumsy formulation will, it is hoped, become clear as we go along.

Starting from scratch in this pioneering project made it mandatory to define the essential aspects of psychoanalytic theory and technique which we wished to pass on to this new breed of practitioners. In that sense we were having to define the canon of a tradition, naming the set of ideas which would carry the essence of and embed the training within psychoanalysis. It also needed to accommodate the special needs of 'counselling' (the official definition of counselling did not appear until several years later, so that also had to be defined), and of our particular student group. A few of them were designated counsellors, but most wanted a counselling perspective that would enhance their effectiveness in their work as social workers, educators, welfare and advisory officers, clergy, tutors, youth workers, nurses, paramedicals, managers. So it had to be something significantly different from classical psychoanalysis, but the alloy should not spoil the pure.

The three of us who designed the original course were all psychoanalytically trained, but from different bases – psychiatry, social work and psychology, and with different pedigrees – Winnicott, Klein and Jung, in so far as people can be defined by their own analyses. From this professional pool it was relatively easy to distil some shared essentials of psychoanalytic theory and practice. We could agree on the 'canon': the formative texts and concepts of psychoanalysis. At the very least we would want students to understand the reality and nature of unconscious processes and the transference in order to use them; we would want to inculcate certain professional and ethical views about the stance of the counsellor, about proper boundaries and constraint in interventions; we would place considerable importance on self-awareness; and in view of the sort of work our students did, we wanted them to be aware of the nature of group and institutional processes, and of the problems of translating clinical ideas into their ordinary working practices.

For some of these aims we could draw on our own training during which we had been given theory seminars and supervision, but others required some innovation. Our setting in the university and our potential population of students meant that we could not require personal therapy as the preferred and traditional method of acquiring self-awareness. Similarly our trainings, which had focused almost exclusively on the one-to-one therapeutic relationship, gave us no inheritance for teaching institutional processes and for helping students to translate the ideas into their particular settings, although we did have some experience of groups and of group relations conferences. The programme that we eventually designed was the answer to the problems posed by these two needs. And it is perhaps what led to our establishing a culture, only part of which could be considered a traditional psychoanalytic training.

The relationship between culture and tradition merits some thought at this point. According to Webster, 'tradition' is defined as 'the oral transmission of information beliefs and customs from ancestors to posterity; an inherited culture or attitude'; while 'culture' is 'the act of developing by education, discipline, and training; or a particular stage in civilization – the integrated pattern of human behaviour that includes thought, speech, action, and artefacts and depends on man's capacity for learning and transmitting knowledge to succeeding generations'. Less formally, a culture is 'the way we do things here' and consists of the values and principles which underlie an enterprise and which inform all its activities. It is transmitted through heroes and myths, rituals and ceremonies, attitudes and standards. Being historically established, the signs of the culture are sometimes more accessible than their meanings and origins, which often settle into the unconscious of the organization.

It is not clear whether the founders of organizations deliberately set out to create a culture, but it is observed that cultures form around 'critical incidents' as solutions to problems. They originate and are reinforced because of their power to reduce anxiety, release emotions, or achieve results (Schein 1985). In our case, the core values and principles did function as a raft of safety in the sea of detailed considerations and tendentious differences, particularly when we went on to refine and design subsequent courses and to entrust them to the second generation of course tutors. These definitions suggest that tradition is both a constituent and a conveyor of a culture. It is tempting to regard the terms as interchangeable, all the more so since apparently our course culture arose out of the psychoanalytic traditions, but came to be conveyed as part of the same analytic tradition. The sought-for integrity of form and content makes it very difficult to pull the thread out of the woven fabric, but I shall return to this problem later.

Our course programme, as it has been gradually refined through experience, consists of five components. Four of them – the theory seminars, case discussion, practical workshops in counselling skills and processes, and an experiential group – occur on every day that the course meets (once a week for two academic years). The fifth, a group relations week, comes in the summer between the two years of the course.

The encompassing frame, however, is that the course should be regarded as a developing institution in its own right, and all the events in the life of the institution would themselves be available for learning through the experience of them. We presumed that the students would naturally be having emotional responses to the learning programme (both the content and the components, for instance hearing about the 'good enough mother' in a seminar or being in a case discussion group) and we also presumed that the events in the course's life-cycle would parallel events in the lifetime of individuals. So if we could grasp the opportunities presented and work with them, whatever the students could learn in the here-and-now about themselves and the processes could be applied to their understanding of their clients and other aspects of their work. Some of these events are:

Beginnings: dealing with expectations, the process of joining and forming new relationships and new working groups, anxiety about what will unfold and their capacity to manage the demands, feelings about exclusion and inclusion arising from the selection process, problems about attachment.

Endings: mourning, gratitude and regret, hopes for the future.

Breaks: going away and coming back in predictable and unpredictable ways.

Authority issues: in relation to the staff as teachers and assessors, to the rules and regulations of the university; becoming authoritative themselves.

Work: learning blocks, establishing effective work habits, meeting course demands, potency and creativity.

Assessment: competition, envy, rivalry, facing individual differences, fear of success and failure.

Decision-making: initiative, leadership, choosing and the consequences, taking responsibility.

Group life: balancing the needs of the individual and the group; anxiety about working in groups; dealing with fantasies about peer groups.

Personal events: responses to the material of the course as it touched their histories, the impact on the group of any of the many things that can happen to individuals (dropping out, marriage, bereavement, having children, illness, divorce, job change) and between individuals (love, hate, rivalry, sexuality, support, co-operation) in the span of two years.

The course as a whole: each of which has a particular atmosphere and dynamic determined by its composition and the state of the world in which it is happening.

Spaces for this reflection on experience are built into the programme through the weekly experiential group, which is described as a place for students to work on the meaning of what they are learning and its impact on themselves and their work. There are also regular 'large group' meetings of the whole course – of students, staff, and secretary – where we can track, at conscious and unconscious levels, the 'state of affairs' at that point in the cycle of the course, using the immediate feelings and phantasies to illuminate a particular aspect of experience and attempting to understand how these may be affecting the learning potential for individuals and the group as a whole. Students also have regular individual tutorials where they discuss their experience of the course. But there is no guarantee that feelings can be held until one of those spaces arrives: the material of the theoretical seminars is, after all, the stuff of emotional life, and it is difficult to talk about it, even in highly abstract theoretical language without stirring up a miasma of feelings from the personal histories of the students and indeed their feelings within the course in the transference.

And here we come up against something of a contradiction or paradox. It is clearly a part of the culture of the course and a demand of the counselling role that the students be aware of their feelings. Students, however, are not clients. The experiential groups are not therapy groups, and attempts to use them as such meet with dismal failure and dissatisfaction. The staff are not therapists to the students, yet they are therapists, and cannot help seeing something of the students' unconscious processes as they are enacted on the course. So how does the line get drawn when the students are actively encouraged to express and explore their feelings and their transferences within the course and yet are not allowed to be clients, and the tutors are not allowed to make a directly therapeutic response to the distress or resistance that may ensue? Within the framework of the course, the desirable answer to that question is that every student discovers the answer through testing the limits of the personal–professional boundary as part of the professional learning. In client work counsellors need to recognize and cope with the feelings aroused within themselves by the client's material. Although they use their feelings to understand the client, on the whole their own feelings have to remain held, invisible, a servant to the process; so the course becomes a place of rehearsal for being aroused and contained at the same time. This is one element of what is meant by students learning as they learn.

Tutors also have to learn where to draw the line, and we have a general guide-line that personal matters can be legitimately pursued so long as they illuminate or explain a student's response to or difficulty with the learning or counselling role; when, however, it is evident that the student is locked into a transference which is meant to repair a past injury but is wilfully reinforcing that negative experience, then it is time to recommend personal therapy. Indeed, another desirable outcome of the paradox is that the students will deal with the tension for themselves and will see the need to embark on personal therapy as the proper place for working through the more personal or unconscious matters thrown up for them in their work and in the course, rather than having to have it pointed out to them by tutors as a recommendation shading into a warning of failure.

THE LEARNING OF FACTS

It can be imagined that this kind of learning does not fit easily into the tradition of an academic department, nor indeed with the expectations of students enrolling on a university course, so perhaps it is useful to pause to consider the business of learning. It is convenient to begin by drawing a distinction between two kinds of teaching and learning, which we may call academic and experiential, although such a distinction is arbitrary. 'Academic' learning refers to gaining knowledge about something in a rational and orderly fashion: through lectures, seminars, reading and research, the subject matter is examined, explained, analysed, probed, practised, and evaluated at a distance and impersonally. The primary direction of the flow is from outside to inside: an external item is brought within the person's mind and lodged somewhere in the intellectual structure of existing knowledge. A student's personal and emotional connections and associations may influence its accuracy, where it is lodged, and how it is recalled, but those are definitely secondary. 'Experiential' learning, by contrast, involves developing an insightful appreciation of the relationship between the learner and the subject matter. The starting point is frequently a reaction to an idea or a situation. That reaction is observed and explored for its personal significance before the subject is conceptualized. Here the primary flow is from inside to outside: an existing set of responses is brought to bear on an external subject, the meanings are pursued, and the result is a modification of the existing conceptualization of the subject. In academic learning, sound learning has been deemed to occur if the knowledge can be recalled when it is required; in experiential learning, sound learning means that a situation will be recognized and awareness of how the self and others are likely to act in that situation will enable the situation to be managed more effectively. Emotional sense leads to intelligence.

Generally experiential learning is associated with subjects which involve people and their feelings, while academic learning is regarded as 'right' for the hard subjects, but no subject is exclusively one or the other. Even the most hard of the sciences and fine of the arts benefit from an integration of academic and experiential learning. Here is a lecturer in English literature speaking:

> I was becoming converted to the idea that literature could be taught successfully only if the experience of reading the text could be related to the student's own experience of analogous feelings and situations. The teaching of literature, like the reading of literature, is not what for a long time I presumed it to be – a discipline of subordinating one's subjective responses to an 'objective' reading of the text, an attempt to hear the author's voice unmuffled by the clamour of the reader's ego. A text assumes significance for the reader only if it can enter into the reader's current life and interact with his or her anxieties, memories, hopes, fantasies, desires and the like. So that to read or teach a text entails finding a point of contact between what the writer is actually saying (in so far as this can be ascertained) and whatever elements of personal experience the text brings to life in the reader.

> (Finney 1985: 257)

Everyone's history of schooling is no doubt littered with evidence that if a subject and a learning situation meet a personal need, they will be pursued eagerly and straightforwardly, but if they arouse anxiety our learning will be somehow distorted. The more curious, enthusiastic, and successful we are at something, the more comfortable we are at undertaking the next step; anxiety can spur us on to greater efforts or can disrupt the existing competence. This is so whether or not we are consciously aware of the factors. In order for the integration of learning to occur, we need to be able to see external reality for what it actually is, but we also have to be aware of what that external reality means to us.

It is ironic that major educational transitions occur when the individual's grasp of the relationship between internal and external reality is often tenuous. Formal education begins at latency when the child is learning to yield impulse-driven needs and desires to the more or less immutable demands of external reality. Some never recover the feeling life, and they are left with a bias toward the very rational, common-sense, active approach to living. Others don't achieve a proper containment of feeling, and they never maintain a hard-edged untrammelled relationship with facts and external reality. This is repeated in adolescence, when the balance is again very precarious because of the efflorescence of primitive impulses. Formative decisions about examinations then can confirm the existing style or combat it. Education itself becomes an arena where students attempt to work out their personal conflicts, or, as Hudson (1972) has it, where they pursue their autobiography at the expense of the subject.

Objective and subjective components of learning augment each other so long as they are not confused with one another, and knowledge has a greater chance of being meaningfully acquired if the students can bring facts into a lively relationship with their experience and if they can appreciate how experience and attitudes affect perception of facts. It is important to know a thing, but it is also important to know how it is known.

Thus learning is an ever-reflexive process, very demanding of the students as they engage in the real task of learning real facts, being emotionally available to the impact of the facts, but also being able to think clearly about what is going on while it is happening in the here and now, and able to work through the transference relationships which are set up with the staff and with other students. This means constantly translating back and forth between the personal and impersonal, the direct and distant, the emotional and conceptual, so

that in the end they may understand and understand the understanding. As for the staff, they too have to be actual supervisors,
teachers and group leaders, and attempt to do that while dealing with
the transferences and countertransferences which arise.

We may assume that some of this, at least, goes on for every
student and teacher of any subject, and consciousness of it is not the
sole province of psychoanalysis or the psychoanalytically-aware. In a
course such as ours, however, we make a point of throwing these
processes into high relief as the material of the spaces set aside for
reflection, attempting to demonstrate how psychoanalytic ideas serve
both as a theoretical framework to be learned and taken back into the
student's work place and as a framework for understanding the
experience of learning while it is happening: 'bending the straight
line of life into circles of timeless personal truth' (Finney 1985: 79).

ACQUIRING A PROFESSIONAL IDENTITY

When trying to understand the kinds of individual and group transferences which arise in a course which also has elements of a professional training, it has been useful to refer to psychoanalytic ideas
about adolescence and the processes of establishing a mature identity
and internalizing authority. In no sense are our students chrono-
logically 'adolescent', but they are going through the processes
normally associated with that phase. This is compounded by the fact
that students often come for a training of this sort at a critical point in
their lives, seeking to acquire new power and possibilities for
themselves. They are ready for a personal and professional transforming experience, consciously or unconsciously knowing the kind
of experience they are seeking.

Psychoanalysis has much of great interest to say about the role of
adolescent sexuality, aggression, dependence, curiosity, and the internalized parent and sibling relationships in the context of learning, but
all that is tantalizingly beyond the scope of this chapter. Here it is
germane to concentrate on the particular relationship between
students and those in authority around them and on the transitional
internal process of becoming authoritative in a new sphere. This is a
necessarily ambivalent process since the students are always to some
degree torn between the attractions of innocence and the potential of
being grown up; and this conflict is experienced in the context of the
person's history and the images of adult authority which exist already
in the individual's internal world. The classroom and material of

learning become the arena and vehicle for working out the conflicts, the teachers and other authorities in the setting become the transference objects for the parent-derived images and relationships, and the students will be looking to them to confirm or modify the old patterns. Conversely, the teachers also bring their personal history and internal worlds to bear in transferences and countertransferences to the students individually and symbolically.

For instance, students will look to see whether the 'adults' want them to become authorities in their own right. Winnicott (1971a) wrote about the murder that is inherent in the achievement of adulthood for the adolescent: in order to relinquish childhood, the parent–child relationship has to be sacrificed and a different adult–adult relationship established. This means that the parents have to survive the attack, not abdicate entirely, but rearrange themselves in relation to the child-become-adult. He also related this to democracy (1965), saying that the truly democratic leader is mature enough to gather power on behalf of others and to share that power through delegation to others. Within this transitional process, of course, lurk the dynamics of envy: whether students can allow the teachers to have something to teach and can allow them to want to give; whether teachers can be free enough of envy of youth to allow them to grow and develop, to be as good as or even better than they are in the field of study.

Associated with this, students will look to see whether the adults can tolerate the inevitable mistakes and arrogance of the novice. It seems easy for teachers to be affronted by the clumsy efforts of the beginners and to turn their back on the students with impatience, or to interfere too readily, to try to do it for them, or to impose their own advanced ideas and interests on the embryonic ideas of the student, effectively stealing them for themselves. Indeed, a failed student is often experienced by the teacher as a personal failure, and marginal students create untold anxiety and may only narrowly miss being failed as the teachers worry about whether 'the world' may perceive them to be also incompetent or may identify the poor practice with the actuality of psychoanalytic counselling 'as taught here'. At best, however, teachers will have the knack of beginning anew with the student, apparently re-identifying with the excitement of discovery, sharing and mirroring the effort, the achievement, and the pleasure of learning.

Students will be looking to see whether the adult seems to enjoy and use the authority creatively or whether it is a weapon or a dreadful burden; whether the teachers are refreshed and inspiring or weary and lifeless with their material. Students who have experienced authority as harsh or frail may be afraid to challenge it on the one hand, and may have little incentive to acquire it on the other hand because it seems to be such an unpleasant quality to possess. It is as if the learner is saying, 'I am not going to be like that when I grow up'; rather, they need an ego ideal which will lead them on.

Rebellion and the challenge to authority is an essential element of the learning process. The contest with the teachers has to happen because it is through this struggle that the students discover their ideas, values, standards and limits. For the teacher to give way too easily or to present an adamantine certainty is to deprive the students of the opportunity for these vital discoveries, and to deprive them of their own creativity, triumph, and reassurance about their own capabilities. Through the rebellion and conflict and through being permitted both to succeed and to fail, the student moves from the position of 'them and us' to a positive identification with 'them', although there may not be agreement on all things.

The process of identification through internalization, which results in the student's accomplishing a position of authority through learning, of becoming professional through the course, and which depends heavily on the benignity of these 'adolescent–adult' authority relationships, seems to take place in four stages: innocence, disillusionment, seeking for certainty and internalization (Barker 1982). Many people come into this kind of training with untested notions of what counselling is and phantasies of what it might be. Others may come with the experience of counselling as they have practised it so far, but are perhaps quite unfamiliar with the psychoanalytic approach. These 'lay views' quite quickly come up against some very powerful contradictions from the system of values presented on the course, and nowhere more starkly than in the experiential group on the first day, which focuses on beginnings. It may be their first exposure to the elucidation of unconscious processes. The students may feel like babies: existing skills and beliefs feel devalued, and they feel angry, anxious and confused. Even as they begin to change their image of counselling towards the one presented, they feel inadequate in relation to the staff who embody the skills and who also have the ultimate authority to make the prevailing definitions stick. In this state of disillusionment, they begin to question whether they are on the right course and whether they should be doing counselling at all. Uncomfortable as they are, these kinds of doubts signal the possibility of change and development and herald the next phase of very active attempts to sort things out.

In this phase of seeking to sort out their relationship to the ideas and the staff, students observe the teachers very closely, ask awkward questions, look for conflict among the staff, and attempt to find out in some depth what their underlying assumptions, standards and values are. This investigation goes on at personal and professional levels, and at best is evidence of a very healthy curiosity. It can be an uncomfortable phase for staff because it is a time of criticism and challenge to them about their ideas and their professionalism and their selves, and they have to survive that without humiliating the tender beginners or evading the aggressiveness of the questioning. Through 'mastering' the teachers, as it were, and testing the setting and the concepts, the students' own sense of competence is fostered; having grasped an important aspect of the course in 'figuring out' the staff, the students are reassured about their capacity to apply the ideas they are learning, and can therefore acknowledge their need to learn and can accept the learning opportunities of the course. It is, of course, also a time of testing out the ideas brought into the course from experience or phantasy, and finding out where the discrepancies really lie, finding out what of their own can be retained and what needs to be altered through new learning. A positive outcome of this process is often a creative end-of-course cabaret where the foibles of the staff and of psychoanalysis are fondly woven into skits and songs.

Students who are overwhelmed by disillusionment, however, remain fearful and mistrustful of the staff and can't partake of this essential testing out. Some lash out with angry recriminations, as they perceive the staff to be playing roles, and with talk of brainwashing, since they find the use of the transference relationship as a teaching medium so at odds with their expectations of both teachers and counsellors. Others silently surrender and merely imitate the staff behaviour and values; they are indeed 'playing a role', being compliant in order to be approved and to remain on the course, while all their reservations are retained and entrenched under the surface.

This taking in of the values and standards of the course staff constitutes the process of internalization, that is, being like the staff in most if not all professional respects. This matches the staff process in designing the course, which is not too far from asking, 'What does it take to be like us?' At first the identification is provisional, since many of the doubts about choice, capacity and suitability remain, and the status of experienced practitioner cannot be internalized except as an ego ideal. The more stable internalization comes with the final assessment, during which the students have the opportunity to demonstrate their capability in and a convincing identification with the profession, and there is public recognition of mastery and development. By passing a student through the course the teachers change from assessors to approvers, so the internalized authority also becomes approving and permitting: the assessment signifies that the students have accomplished professionalism to the limits of this particular course. Shedding the student status is in itself a significant step in the process and is very reminiscent of Winnicott's (1971b) ideas about the formation of the self through sorting out what is me and not me within the containing transitional relationship. Identity and authority become almost synonymous; this is particularly pertinent in a professional training because people do go out and say, 'I am a counsellor.' Arriving at this point of internalization is a perilous process, and it almost always involves a crisis of some sort for the student. The crisis may be benign and smooth in the manner of developmental transitions, but it can also be very traumatic, requiring some major internal realignments.

The parallels between the learning situation and the therapeutic relationship during this process of internalization and identification are no doubt obvious, in the way the therapist allows the patient to be 'better' than he is, in the therapeutic excitement of each unique journey of discovery, in the patient's humiliation in needing so much, and in the aggressive investigation of the 'innards' of the analyst at certain phases of the relationship. In this sense the 'traditional' promulgation of psychoanalysis through the analytic family tree (analysts metaphorically beget progeny in the way that parents beget children) is replicated here, and indeed counsellors are identified and categorized by the course they have taken. Bearing in mind that it is not therapy, however, it is perhaps instructive to look at a couple of specific differences.

One of these is selection. It is assumed among trainers that some people will choose to train as a counsellor as a substitute for or a circumvention of personal therapy. Consequently an exploration of motivation is as crucial as it is when taking on a patient or client for an extensive treatment. The paradox of the training being a non-therapy therapeutic experience is set up right at the outset, because the selection interview closely follows a diagnostic interview. Candidates will be asked about their early experience with parents, their experience of learning so far, any personal experience of counselling (or specific avoidance of it), the solidity of current relationships, the current stresses in their lives and the psychological resources they have for managing the impact of the course. They are asked about their work, and are likely to be offered a trial interpretation about countertransference issues as a here-and-now test of their capacity to respond to the spirit of the training and their readiness to choose the psychoanalytic approach in their work. Naturally an interview of this depth makes every candidate a 'suitable case for treatment'.

To be a 'suitable case for training', however, the candidates must satisfy the course staff that they have sufficient capacity to learn using the kind of dimensions that have been the subject of this chapter: in particular, the capacity to let the text 'enter into their current life and interact with their anxieties, memories, hopes, fantasies, desires and the like' while retaining the capacity to learn the text and to think clearly about it at the same time; and a sufficiently mature attitude towards authority to be able to undergo that 'adolescent' transition again, aside, of course, from having the requisite intellectual power to succeed at the academic requirements. Often the deciding factor is a countertransference response on the part of the interviewer: wanting the candidate as a 'good' patient who would be helped rather than as a student who could be helped to learn is a clear negative indicator, ignored at the peril of both student and staff (and even other students). Anyone who creates radically different responses in two interviewers is doubtful. The interviewer has to make a judgement based on experience of the kind and extent of personal difficulty that can be managed within the group and the learning structures provided. For instance, extreme deprivation, a recent significant bereavement, unresolved maternal envy, and deep urges toward manic reparation make a candidate doubtful. On the other hand, anxiety about groups, anxiety about the capacity to learn, inhibited aggression underlying a history of depression and underachievement, and intellectualizing defences usually can be managed within the course because the course structures themselves will be relevant to the personal development ahead. In this sense, the course structures and events may function legitimately as vehicles for personal development.

Once the course is under way, given that every student will experience moments of difficulty with the material and demands of the course, questions arise about how to understand and help the student through these moments without the sanctions and safeties of therapy, especially when the difficulty is a resistance in the transference. The problem for the trainer as for the analyst is that no one can develop anyone except himself or herself; the door to development is locked from the inside. The experiential groups and the individual tutorials can be places to attempt to work with such a resistance, so long as the student and staff both remain sufficiently in touch with the primacy of the learning task (the concept of focal therapy is useful here). But generally speaking the student is necessarily left to work it through in his or her own time, and the staff need to resist the temptation to engage in an overt therapist–patient interaction. The teacher may, however, function silently as an alternative ego or super-ego during the period of working through. In a supervision group, for instance, the supervisor can be experienced as a persecuting super-ego criticizing the relationship between the counsellor and client, but in so far as the case or problem presented by the student is also his or her own problem, the supervisor can function as an auxiliary ego to hold and contain uncertainty and confusion. This is seldom the place for voicing an interpretation, but it is a good place for using the insights of psychoanalysis to behave or speak interpretatively, for instance, by helping the student to elucidate the transference or by setting temporary boundaries to protect the student against the worst effects of a rampant countertransference. A simple supporting or theoretical comment may provide enough structure to free the student to think privately or publicly about the interfering anxiety concerning a case.

When it comes to the assessment, of course, and when the staff perceive that the limit on a student's achievement is the consequence of some unconscious resistance or blind spot, it is extremely difficult to judge an inadequacy based on something that the student by definition can't own or refuses to acknowledge as significant. This is an awful moment of truth, and returns us to the question of tradition.

TRADITION OR INDOCTRINATION?

Through looking at the process of learning and some specific aspects of the course, I have tried to show how it promotes a particular intellectual and technical tradition. As such, it gathers unto itself willing protagonists who find it useful, stimulating and even comforting. This is no different, really, from the way a family gathers its generations around the Christmas tree and passes on its rituals for celebrating the holiday and its tried and tested solutions for enhancing the pleasure and minimizing the conflicts of the occasion. But here the tradition which is transmitted is also used to determine how it is taught and to assess how well the students are performing. The whole system is pretty well wrapped up. That might seem to be the ultimate achievement in tidiness and consistency were it not for the students who fail, who succumb to disillusionment, or otherwise become 'victims of the unfathomable process' (Barham 1984), and who may allege that we are imposing an ideology through forcible indocrination. This is a horrifying thought, since a cherished aspect of analytic work is freeing patients from the constraints of their individual historical indoctrinations so that they may make genuine choices in the present, and since a central aspiration of the course is that people develop – not lose – their capacity to think; but the issue deserves some thought, without, one hopes, the tactic of simply climbing back on to the raft of safety in the face of contention. It is important to be able to understand whether a 'deviant' student is being resistant or creative; it is important to know whether 'because it works for me' is the best or worst possible answer to the question 'why psychoanalysis?'

We hold in good faith the belief that the explanatory power of psychoanalysis is great: not just about patients, but about social, historical, artistic and scientific phenomena (notwithstanding a body of research that fails to confirm the universal effectiveness of psychoanalysis as a mode of treatment). Freud stands among the crowd of great classics – the Bible, Plato, Homer, Dante, Shakespeare, Dickens, Newton, Einstein, Mendel, Marx and Darwin – which are presumed to be the best that have been known and thought and which help us to understand the history of western civilization. Within psychoanalysis, the texts of Freud, Klein, Jung and Winnicott are chosen as the canon not because they are the last word, but because they were the first and fundamental words. They reveal not only the thoughts but also the thinking behind the thoughts which enable us to place psychoanalysis and its own development in its evolving social context.

So, too, is the training designed in good faith as a sturdy and consistent holding environment within the safety of which people might be enabled to learn some difficult things. They may even be universal things in so far as the experiences generated within the training can be taken as essential truths about human nature and human interactions. The boundary of the container does not in any way act as a preserving ring against the intrusions of today's preoccupations, be those racism, the need for a qualification in the market economy of counselling, or whatever. Such leakage curiously increases the sense of safety within, because it signifies that the container is not a prison within which the only allowable understanding of human 'truths' is the one already known. The shape of the experiential space is determined by the principles of psychoanalysis and the method of understanding the experience that occurs there is also an application of psychoanalysis. Because of this it may be difficult to evaluate objectively the origins and adequacy of the method, but it does not necessarily invalidate it nor limit the exploration that can occur.

Winnicott (1971c) drew our attention to the importance of allowing objects to be real and separate from us; transitional space is vital, but if objects remain in the realm of our omnipotent projections they are of no use to us in any creative process. The experiential spaces are actually nothing more than transitional spaces where students work out and play with their relationship to ideas and experiences. However, human beings are what we understand them to be, and, in a sense, psychoanalysis is what we understand it to be at any moment in time – an ambiguity of status which it shares with all the disciplines which attempt to study people: anthroplogy, sociology, philosophy, intellectual history, and so on. The human world is a world of culturally determined meaning, so in a real way we might be trapped for ever in our omnipotent projections. To escape from this ever-reflexive spiral, it may be helpful to adopt a perspective from a different but analogous discipline: autobiography.

In *The Inner I* (1985) Finney writes about autobiography as a literary form and as a source of information about the author. A reader in search of reality or truth or understanding of the author can ransack the text for the facts, events, and people which make up the life, but in fact greater understanding of the person is derived from trying to apprehend the meaning which has been attributed to those facts, events, and people in the account of the life. This comes not just from what the autobiographer says, but also from the literary features – the style, language, form, images, etc. – which are part of the data because they indicate how the author has shaped his own life. In other words, the way a life is chronicled exposes more of the author than he can consciously express or control, and the underlying biases and desires, 'the distorting mirror of the self-image' are revealed. Given this, the reality of the life, the truth about himself, is a construction that reflects the moment of writing.

Furthermore, the act of writing the autobiography becomes part of the life that is being written about: the story changes in the course of the telling and as a result of the telling. In the tension between being the protagonist and the intellectual researcher in search of the protagonist who was, but no longer is, the same person, the writer rectifies and refashions the past. Finney suggests that autobiographers cannot be asked to tell the factual truth; it is only possible to ask them to present life as they perceive it.

While the analogy is not perfect, there are ways in which this training is akin to writing an autobiography. We can only present psychoanalysis as we perceive it at the moment. Although eyebrows may fly up at the notion of reshaping the past in the light of the present, it is true that we understand Freud's work differently as we continually re-evaluate and reinterpret nineteenth-century Vienna and the travail of the 1930s and 1940s, and as different social and human issues preoccupy us and test the explanatory power of psychoanalysis. This enables us to 'put him in his place' and is an antidote to both idealization and petrification.

It is equally true that as a 'reader' a member of the course can observe not only what is said about psychoanalysis but also how the form and structure of the course – the 'literary features' – embody the ideas and reveal the biases and desires, so they have the data for evaluating the validity of the 'text'. As students and users of psychoanalysis they are part of the story and how they do that may change the story itself. At some critical point in becoming identified with it, however, the member ceases to be a character and becomes a protagonist in a new life history. The problem of trying to understand it out there becomes the problem of trying to make sense of it from within.

Furthermore, since autobiography is not just the history of the protagonist, but is also a history of its time, a central problem for both writer and reader is to discover the extent to which the writer is a product of, an influencer of, or independent of prevailing social trends. Analogously, it is interesting to puzzle at how much the revision of 'basic Freud' by all the substantial thinkers up to and including the present are products and influencers of society and how much the revision has evolved by its own internal developmental needs. Whatever the answer to that puzzle is, surely psychoanalysis can be conceived of as a story of a life in the world. Inevitably we go back to the beginning to discover how it got to be where it is now, and in so doing we say as much about ourselves now as we do about it then.

Finney draws an interesting distinction between the egocentric autobiographers, who place themselves at the centre of the world while still acknowledging the historical context, and the narcissistic authors who believe themselves to be the only worthwhile objects of interest and take no account of historical and social circumstances. It could be said that 'because it works for me' as the answer to the question 'why psychoanalysis?' is a mere outcropping of narcissism. But the fact of the matter is, that although Freud happened upon psychoanalysis as a solution that resolved a problem he had, the solution has an internal logic which has stood up across an immense variety of experience. It has worked for untold others, partly because individuals have an internal logic which is waiting to be happened upon, but surely because psychoanalysis has taken a lively cognizance of changing historical and social circumstances, albeit in an egocentric way.

It now begins to be safe to say that if it doesn't work for particular students, the problem lies in the students, not in the method. The resistance is revealed in what they say about their experience; usually it is some form of 'I am held back and victimized by these ideas', and they seek refuge in the safety of their pre-existing notions, not unlike the child who refuses spinach having never or barely tasted it because it is thought to have a nasty taste. This is truly different from the 'deviant' student who says, 'I am frustrated by the unsatisfactoriness of these ideas' and is urged forward to discover more about that frustration and may in the process find a new, more satisfactory, idea. This actually is the history of the development of psychoanalytic ideas, as within the core principles and values new problems generate new solutions and, perforce, tweak the culture and the tradition.

Psychoanalysis does allow for its own revision, and this sheds a final ray of light on training. Learning is a matter of finding the balance between tradition and inventiveness. To revisit an earlier theme: a healthy outcome of the struggle between adolescent and adult is that the new adult is free to leave home, that is, to challenge the tradition and create something more contemporary. In order to challenge, however, they have to know enough of the culture and tradition to know how it got to be the way it is. Only then is the separation a mature (as contrasted to a petulant) action, and the newly created life carries within it significant elements of what is being ostensibly left behind. Somehow this transforms a psychological experience into a historical fact in a way that resembles resolving the transference. Having seen our students through the intellectual and emotional childhood of their professional life, we actually don't want them to go away and be like us. We want them to resolve their transference and go away and be themselves as they have become, so that they can be the new transmitters of the tradition which now encompasses their experience.

An eminent analyst once made the off-hand comment that psychoanalysis is an incurable disease, meaning that once we have experienced it and its efficacy, we are condemned to an ever-restless attempt to understand ourselves and our world using the concepts of psychoanalysis. This is an alarming thought, but true: leaving aside the technical specificity of the consulting room, psychoanalysis is not something one does; it is a way of life. Living in and living out this tradition is what makes the course a transforming experience for the students.

REFERENCES

Barham, P. (1984) 'Cultural forms and psychoanalysis: some problems', in B. Richards (ed.) *Capitalism and Infancy*, London: Free Association Books.

Barker, M. (1982) 'Through experience toward theory: a psychodynamic contribution of social work education', *Issues in Social Work Education* 2(1): 3–25.

Finney, B. (1985) *The Inner I*, London: Faber & Faber.

Freud, S. (1919) 'Lines of advance in psycho-analytic therapy', in *Standard Edition of the Complete Psychological Works of Sigmund Freud*, 24 vols, 1953–74, edited by J. Strachey, London: Hogarth Press (SE) 17.

—— (1926) 'The question of lay analysis', in SE 20.

Hudson, L. (1972) *The Cult of the Fact*, London: Jonathan Cape.

Schein, S. (1985) 'How culture forms: theoretical perspectives', in *Organizational Culture and Leadership*, New York: Jossey Bass.

Winnicott, D. (1965) 'Some thoughts on the meaning of the word democracy', in *The Family and Individual Development*, London: Tavistock Publications.

—— (1971a) 'Contemporary concepts of adolescent development', in *Playing and Reality*, London: Tavistock Publications.

—— (1971b) 'Transitional objects and transitional phenomena', in *Playing and Reality*, London: Tavistock Publications.

—— (1971c) 'The use of an object and relating through identifications', in *Playing and Reality*, London: Tavistock Publications.

Chapter 2

'Infidel Jew'
Freud, Jewish ritual and psychoanalysis

David Aberbach

Was du ererbt von deinen Vätern hast
Erwirb es, um es zu besitzen.

What you inherit from your fathers
Earn it first to make it yours.
(Goethe, *Faust*, Part I, Scene i)

From the standpoint of traditional Judaism – Judaism, that is, as a religious way of life – Sigmund Freud (1856–1939) was a heretic and a self-confessed one at that: he was concerned less with providence than with secular enlightenment, less with Jewish religious and national consciousness than with psychoanalytic insight, less with the continuation and growth of the Jewish religious tradition than with the universal brotherhood of man governed by reason. Freud was the first in his family to have the choice of how to define himself as a Jew. Unlike his rabbinic ancestors, Freud devoted his life not to the idea that the Jews are divinely chosen as 'a light to the nations' but to the principle that all people, the Jews included, are driven by the same fundamental instincts. Freud was raised in an assimilated Jewish environment which extolled the virtues of enlightenment (or Haskalah in Hebrew) and, while retaining some traditional practices, rejected rabbinic Judaism with its emphasis on Talmudic law as being narrow, backward and largely antithetical to the modern world and to scientific progress. Judging from Freud's own writings, anti-Semitism and the attraction of secular enlightenment, far more than the healthy, vibrant side of the rabbinic tradition, drove him to succeed in the non-Jewish world.

At the time of Freud's birth, Judaism was defined largely in religious terms, and the majority of Jews, particularly in Eastern Europe, expressed their Jewishness mainly through ritual observance.

Freud's generation had access as never before to higher education, which at the time did not sit well with Jewish religious practices; these maintained family and communal cohesion but set the Jews apart from the Christian world. These practices include: regular prayer and study in Hebrew and Aramaic, the observance of the Sabbath, festivals and dietary laws, and the maintenance of customs such as circumcision, the bar mitzvah, rabbinic weddings and funerals. As a result, generational tension, conflict and guilt were at an especially high pitch, and this was true in Freud's case, as is revealed most strikingly in *The Interpretation of Dreams*.

Freud's family background – both his parents came from orthodox Jewish homes in Eastern European towns – was a source of strength, energy, and conflict, particularly with his father. In *From Oedipus to Moses*, the French psychoanalyst Marthe Robert argues persuasively that Freud's troubled bond with his father had a specifically Jewish side and deeply coloured his psychoanalytic theories. Jakob Freud, like many other Jewish fathers at the time, 'was too much of a Jew to break with a bloodless tradition in which his children saw nothing but the empty aping of ritual, but not enough of a Jew to hand down a possibility of authentic self-contained and self-justifying existence' (Robert 1976: 9–10). Freud regarded being Jewish as a training in embattled minority views (Freud 1926: 274), and it may be that as founder of a new tradition he had to play down the virtues of the old. Yet the evidence seems to be that Freud knew precious little about these virtues, for religious Judaism as he saw it at home was a thing of shreds and patches, abhorrent in its hypocrisy (Aberbach 1980). Freud might have been referring to himself when he wrote that a religion 'must be hard and unloving to those who do not belong to it' (Freud 1921: 98). Absent in Freud's conception of Jewish ritual and learning is its warm, healthy, life-giving side, enabling the Jews to survive hatred and persecution through the ages. His sense of what it meant to be a practising Jew was inauthentic and confused and led in the end to his notorious dismissal of Judaism in *Moses and Monotheism*.

What is known of Freud's religious background? Revealingly little.[1] Jones (1957: 350) writes of Freud's parents, 'Whatever may have been their custom previously, after coming to Vienna [in 1859] they dispensed with the Jewish dietary observances and with most of the customary rituals.' The family continued to celebrate Passover and Jakob Freud conducted the *seder* by heart. To the end of his life he studied the Talmud and read a great deal of Hebrew literature (Heller 1956: 419). Freud himself mentions none of this in his surviving

writings, nor that he himself in his youth was 'conversant with all
Jewish customs and festivals [and] had of course been taught Hebrew'
(Jones 1953: 19, 21). What is clear is his almost total non-observance,
already as young man, and his general failure to recognize the life-
affirming role of religious ritual, which he dismissed as 'antiquated
nuisance' (ibid.: 351). His dominant view was that religion is a form
of immaturity (Freud 1927: 53), and he describes neurosis as 'an
individual religiosity and religion as a universal obsessional neurosis'
(Freud 1907: 126–7). While his father might have fasted on Tisha
B'Av (the anniversary of the destruction of the Temple in Jerusalem)
and Yom Kippur, Freud himself did not. He wrote to his fiancée on
8 September 1883, a few weeks before Yom Kippur, 'Am I to fast at
Yom Kippur . . .? Surely not' (E. L. Freud (ed.) 1960: 55). The idea
of being married under a *chupa* (canopy) by a rabbi was 'anathema' to
Freud (Jones 1953: 140). The rite of circumcision is denigrated by
Freud as a relic of castration, a possible cause of anti-Semitism
(Freud 1939: 91, 123). Freud's cremation in London was a final act
of defiance against Jewish ritual, as cremation is against Jewish law.

Freud's family life was devoid of Jewish ritual. His wife, who came
from a very religious home, would have liked to observe some of the
rituals: 'In 1938 Martha and Freud were still carrying on a long-
standing humorous (and yet serious) argument over the issue of
lighting candles on Friday evenings; Martha joked at Freud's
monstrous stubbornness which prevented her from performing the
ritual, while he firmly maintained that the practice was foolish and
superstitious' (Roazen 1975: 48). Jones writes that after Freud's
death 'she would find interest in discussing Jewish customs and
festivals with anyone of a similar cast of thought' (Jones 1953: 152).
Freud's children consequently knew very little about Judaism.
Freud's son Martin tells of his maternal grandmother, Emmeline:
'She stayed with us occasionally and on Saturdays we used to hear her
singing Jewish prayers in a small but firm and melodious voice. All of
this, strangely enough in a Jewish family, seemed alien to us children
who had been brought up without any instruction in Jewish ritual'
(M. Freud 1957: 14).

In this way, the Freud family, in common with many Western
European Jewish families at the time, abandoned Jewish tradition. It
may be that psychoanalysis, with its own ritual and dogma, its stress
upon the inner life, its faith in the potential improvability of man, in
some ways represents the return of the repressed tradition in altered
secular form. Freud's theories themselves alert us to the potential

significance of the abandoned religious way of life which, perhaps like early memories, cannot be forgotten without trace or substitute. 'It is typically Jewish', wrote Freud to his son Ernst on 17 January 1938, 'not to renounce anything and replace what is lost' (E. L. Freud (ed.): 440). In view of the massive literature on Freud, it is extraordinary that the most basic information pertaining to his Jewish practices and education is almost totally lacking, and the fragments which have survived usually contradict one another. For example, there is Freud's self-description as 'godless' (Gay 1987: 37, 38), as an 'infidel Jew' (Freud 1927: 170); yet, Roazen (1975) points out, he could still argue the existence of God and see religion as having a positive function:

> Despite his scepticism, with individual patients in treatment Freud felt that religion might serve as a constructive resolution of inner conflicts. He even sometimes regretted the increasing inability of modern man to believe in God.
>
> (ibid.: 23–4)

'Un-Jewish' was Freud's description of his education (E. L. Freud (ed.): 394); how does this square with the fact that he was sent to synagogue classes (Jones 1957: 350) and that the closest adult friend of his youth was Samuel Hammerschlag, who taught him Hebrew and Bible at school? 'He has been touchingly fond of me for years', said Freud of Hammerschlag, 'there is such a secret sympathy between us that we can talk intimately together. He always regards me as his son' (Jones 1953: 163). If his education was truly as 'un-Jewish' as he alleges, how was it that for his thirty-fifth birthday his father presented him with a Bible with a Hebrew inscription: 'Thou hast seen in this Book the vision of the Almighty, thou hast heard willingly, thou hast done and hast tried to fly high on the wings of the Holy Spirit' (Jones 1953: 19). Was there a touch of disinguousness in Freud in claiming to be uncertain of the meaning of the word Menorah (Jones 1957: 350), yet able to allude with brilliant aptness on the eve of his departure from Nazi-occupied Vienna in 1938 to the rabbinic legend of Rabbi Yohanan ben Zakkai (ibid.: 221)?

As for change in Freud's religious observances and spiritual life, there is virtually no information. How did Freud pass from the stage at which, as he admits with no explanation in *The Interpretation of Dreams*, he was 'content with *spiritual* food' (Freud 1899: 208) to become absolutely and profoundly irreligious and critically negative about religion in old age?

How did he come to express such diametrically opposite views towards Judaism as those in his letter to his fiancée of 23 July 1882 and in *Moses and Monotheism*? In the letter, he praises his betrothed's grandfather, Chief Rabbi of Hamburg, and expresses sympathy for the life-affirming practice of ritual blessing: 'the law commands the Jew . . . to say grace over every fruit which makes him aware of the beautiful world in which it is grown. The Jew is made for joy and joy for the Jew' (E. Freud (ed.): 21). In *Moses and Monotheism*, in contrast, Freud dismisses religion as a compulsive neurosis and Judaism as a 'father-religion' killed by Christianity, the 'son-religion', making Judaism a 'fossil':

> Judaism had become a religion of the father; Christianity became a religion of the son. The old God, the Father, fell back behind Christ; Christ, the Son, took his place just as every son had hoped to do in primeval times . . . and from that time on the Jewish religion was, to some extent, a fossil.
>
> (Freud 1939: 88)

And how does one account for the extremes in Freud's attitudes towards his Jewish origins, veering as he did between desiring baptism to Christianity and martyrdom for the Jewish cause? Jewish religious ritual as he saw it in Vienna of the late nineteenth century was so repugnant to him that he actually discussed with his friend and colleague Josef Breuer the possibility of conversion to Christianity, rather than undergo the ordeal of a traditional Jewish wedding (Jones 1953: 167). (When Freud's friend, the Swiss pastor Oskar Pfister, declared to him in 1918 that his work showed that he was the best of Christians, Freud did not object, though his daughter, Anna, found this idea incomprehensible.) At the other extreme is his remarkable declaration to his fiancée on 2 February 1886: 'I have often felt as though I had inherited all the defiance and all the passion with which our ancestors defended their Temple and could gladly sacrifice my life for one great moment in history' (E. L. Freud (ed.): 202).

Among Freud's reasons for destroying his own early letters, diaries and other memorabilia of childhood – the most recent biography of Freud (Gay 1988) covers Freud's childhood and youth in under twenty pages – was a not-unjustified fear that public knowledge of his personal background and motives might undermine the credibility of his new 'science'; he did not want this to be dismissed as a 'Jewish national affair' (Abraham and Freud (eds): 34). Freud's father belonged to a transitional generation in that he was born into a strictly orthodox Jewish Eastern European environment, abandoning his orthodoxy as a young man and marrying Freud's mother (his third wife) in a reform synagogue, but never totally turning away from Jewish religious life. He never went as far as some who, like Heine, saw Judaism less as a religion than as a misfortune and won their 'entrance ticket' to European civilization through baptism. But the emotional and cultural upheaval caused by his move from a largely rural Hasidic world, wholly Jewish and dominated by rabbinic authority, to a secular, sceptical, enlightened, anti-religious existence in one of the great European cities, seething with chauvinism and anti-Semitism, was inherited by Freud.[2] Uprooted from Jewish orthodoxy, yet not accepted in the Gentile world, Freud created an intellectual territory of his own which transcended and implicitly rejected both religious parochialism and racism.

The virulently anti-Semitic nature of his environment, a strong dose of Jewish self-hate, and revulsion at Jewish religious ritual were all important factors both in Freud's neglect of his religious heritage and, presumably, in his creation of psychoanalysis. As we have seen, he rarely acknowledged the normative, healthy aspects of the religious tradition he rejected as a collective neurosis, or publicized his enormous debt to it. In particular, Freud was a product of an educational tradition sustained by the Jewish religion, which for hundreds of years had made the Jews the only large group in Europe among whom illiteracy was practically unknown. The psychoanalytic role which Freud created for himself was in some ways similar to that of East European rabbis, who often advised members of their congregations in their personal lives, and had close circles of adherents. While he had probably inherited his prodigious memory and analytic ability from his rabbinic ancestors, Freud ignored the practical importance of the Talmudic background to his way of thinking (Frieden 1990). Kafka once wrote that Freud's works are a continuation of the Talmud, though there is not a single reference to the Talmud in the twenty-four volumes of Freud's *Collected Works*. (Freud does incidentally refer to the Holy Ghost.) The intellectual milieu in which Freud lived was hostile to the Talmud as the source of rabbinic authority. This authority was not so much associated with family and social stability as linked with Jew-hatred as well as with superstition and the unscientific, which had been rejected in favour of rationalism and secular enlightenment.

These are, of course, only some of the possible reasons why Freud's religious background was important in his creation of psychoanalysis.[3]

It may be that, as in the case of other thinkers, such as Marx or Durkheim, the phantom way of life was transformed into a universal system of thought in which the alienation and the disabilities involved in being Jewish could be overcome, and the causes of all forms of social malaise, including racial hatred, could be subjected to rational enquiry, and like illnesses, be treated and cured.

Still, what is unusual about Freud in the context of his time is not the denial but the extent to which he asserts his Jewish origins – in a social rather than religious sense – especially in response to anti-Semitism.[4] Among Freud's interpretations of his own dreams, the clearest and most moving are often those reflecting his Jewishness; some of them, particularly those concerning Rome, Freud connects with his father's humiliation by an anti-Semite. Anti-Semitism, far more than anything positive in the Jewish religious tradition, gave Freud a sense of identity as a Jew (see Aberbach 1980). This point cannot be overstressed, as psychoanalysis is an implicit attack on anti-Semitism, and on human prejudice in general; Freud's central assumption is that all men are driven by the same instincts and are, in a sense, equally wicked. Therefore it is ludicrous for any set of men to regard themselves as racially superior.

Once actually in Rome (which he visited many times after completing *The Interpretation of Dreams*), Freud seems to have felt most acutely the extent of his break with his rabbinic ancestors, as he stood in front of Michelangelo's Moses in the church of San Pietro in Vincoli.[5] Here, as he revealed in a startling confession, he saw himself not in the role of the biblical lawgiver or creator of a new Torah, but as part of the rabble who abandon the true God and his eternal Word:

> Sometimes I have crept cautiously out of the half-gloom of the interior as though I myself belonged to the mob upon whom his eye is turned – the mob which can hold fast no conviction, which has neither faith nor patience, and which rejoices when it has regained its illusory idols.
>
> (Freud 1914: 213)

However bold and fearless Freud was in defending his people against anti-Semitic onslaughts, he saw himself as an 'infidel Jew', a heretical conformist in joining the mutiny against Jewish tradition. In a different age, he might have been a new Moses, continuer of a great religious tradition. Instead, he founded a breakaway system of thought which, ultimately perhaps, could best survive and flourish within the very tradition which it set out to undermine.

NOTES

1 See, for example, Aron 1956–7, Berkower 1969, Gay 1987, Gordis 1975, Grollman 1965, Loewenberg 1971, Simon 1957 and Vogel 1975, who, however insightful, for the most part draw on the same limited sources. For further bibliography on Freud and Judaism, see Miller 1981.
2 On Freud and the crisis of Jewish adaptation to modern life, see, among others, Blatt 1988, Cuddihy 1974, Gay 1987 and Heer 1972.
3 For full-length interpretations of Judaism and its possible effects upon psychoanalysis, see Klein 1985 and Robert 1976.
4 On Freud's Zionist sympathies, see Falk 1978 and Loewenberg 1970.
5 On Freud and Moses, see Bergmann 1976, Handelman 1982, Rice 1990 and Yerushalmi 1991.

REFERENCES

Aberbach, D. (1980) 'Freud's Jewish problem', *Commentary* 69 (6): 35–9.
Abraham, H. C. and Freud, E. (eds) (1965) *A Psychoanalytic Dialogue: the Letters of Sigmund Freud and Karl Abraham, 1907–1926*, London: Hogarth Press.
Aron, W. (1956–7) 'Notes on Sigmund Freud's ancestry and Jewish contacts', *YIVO Annual of Jewish Social Science* 11: 286–95.
Bergmann, M. S. (1976) 'Moses and the evolution of Freud's Jewish identity', *The Israel Annals of Psychiatry and Related Disciplines* 14: 3–26.
Berkower, L. (1969) 'The enduring effect of the Jewish tradition upon Freud', *American Journal of Psychiatry* 125: 1067–73.
Blatt, D. S. (1988) 'The development of the hero: Sigmund Freud and the reformation of the Jewish tradition', *Psychoanalysis and Contemporary Thought* 11: 639–703.
Cuddihy, J. M. (1974) *The Ordeal of Civility: Freud, Marx, Levi-Strauss, and the Jewish Struggle with Modernity*, New York: Basic Books.
Falk, A. (1978) 'Freud and Herzl', *Contemporary Psychoanalysis* 14: 357–87.
Freud, E. L. (ed.) (1960) *The Letters of Sigmund Freud*, trans. T. and J. Stern, New York: Basic Books.
Freud, M. (1957) *Glory Reflected*, London: Angus & Robertson.
Freud, S. (1899) *The Interpretation of Dreams, Standard Edition of the Complete Psychological Works of Sigmund Freud*, 24 vols, 1953–74, edited by J. Strachey, London: Hogarth Press (SE) 4, 5.
—— (1907) 'Obsessive acts and religious practices', in SE 9: 117–27.
—— (1914) 'The Moses of Michelangelo', in SE 13: 211–36.
—— (1921) 'Group psychology and the analysis of the ego', in SE 18: 67–143.
—— (1926) 'Address to the Society of B'nai Brith', in SE 20: 273–4.
—— (1927) *The Future of an Illusion*, SE 21: 5–56.
—— (1939) *Moses and Monotheism*, SE 23: 7–137.
Frieden, K. (1990) *Freud's Dream of Interpretation*, Albany: State University of New York Press.
Gay, P. (1987) *A Godless Jew: Freud, Theism and the Making of Psychoanalysis*, New Haven, Conn.: Yale University Press.

——— (1988) *Freud: a Life for Our Time*, New York: Norton.

Gordis, R. (1975) 'The two faces of Freud', *Judaism* 24: 194–200.

Grollman, E. A. (1965) *Judaism in Sigmund Freud's World*, New York: Appleton-Century.

Haddad, G. (1981) *L'Enfant illegitime: Sources talmidiques de la psychoanalyse*, Paris: Hachette.

Handelman, S. A. (1982) *The Slaying of Moses: the Emergence of Rabbinic Interpretation in Modern Literary Theory*, Albany, NY: State University of New York Press.

Heer, F. (1972) 'Freud, the Viennese Jew', in J. Miller (ed.) *Freud: the Man, his World, his Influence*, London: Weidenfeld & Nicolson.

Heller, J. B. (1956) 'Freud's mother and father', *Commentary* 21 (5): 418–21.

Jones, E. (1953–7) *Sigmund Freud: Life and Work*, 3 vols, vol. 1 (1953), vol. 2 (1955), vol. 3 (1957) New York: Basic Books.

Klein, D. (1985) *Jewish Origins of the Psychoanalytic Movement*, Chicago: University of Chicago Press.

Loewenberg, P. (1970) 'A hidden Zionist theme in Freud's "My son, the Myops . . ." dream', *Journal of the History of Ideas* 31: 129–32.

——— (1971) ' "Sigmund Freud as a Jew": a study in ambivalence and courage', *Journal of the History of the Behavioural Sciences* 7: 363–9.

Miller, J. (1981) 'Interpretations of Freud's Jewishness, 1924–1974', *Journal of the History of the Behavioural Sciences* 18: 357–74.

Rice, E. (1990) *Freud and Moses: The Long Journey Home*, Albany, NY: State University of New York Press.

Roazen, P. (1975) *Freud and His Followers*, New York: Alfred A. Knopf.

Robert, M. (1976) *From Oedipus to Moses: Freud's Jewish Identity*, trans. R. Manheim, Garden City, New York: Anchor Books.

Simon, E. (1957) 'Sigmund Freud, the Jew', *Leo Baeck Institute Year Book* 2: 270–305.

Vogel, L. (1975) 'Freud and Judaism: an analysis in the light of his correspondence', trans. M. Sachs, *Judaism* 24: 181–93.

Yerushalmi, Y. H. (1991) *Freud's Moses: Judaism Terminable and Interminable*, New Haven and London: Yale University Press.

Chapter 3

Tradition and experience
The psyche in the realm of the sacred in Jungian thought

David Hewison

Vocatus atque non vocatus deus aderit.

Invoked or not invoked, the god will be present.

(Erasmus)

When C. G. Jung says that 'the gods have become diseases' (Jung 1957: 37) he is indicating a view of the psyche radically different from that found in contemporary psychiatry or psychology, and different even from that found in psychoanalysis. He is challenging notions that psychotherapy can be a secular matter concerned only with a quasi-medical model of 'cure', and thus divorced from an examination of the sacred, and of its role in both psychopathology and technique. At the same time, he is raising questions as to not only the role and place of religious tradition in efforts to find meaning in life, but their very efficacy; the gods are now symptoms because western traditional religions are failing to contain and make comprehensible those manifestations of the psyche that lie in the realm of the sacred. For Jung, just as for Tertullian, the early Church father, the psyche is *naturaliter religiosa*, naturally religious.

This chapter endeavours to investigate Jung's own, and post-Jungian, attempts to grapple with some of the issues arising from such a view. It begins with an investigation into Jung's views on tradition in general and finds that he offers us a model of tradition that is based on a tension between the immediacy and fragility of experience, and the familiar and profound distillations of our cultural heritage; it is a tension that gives tradition itself an ambivalent character.

The chapter then goes on to look at the nature of the sacred as seen by two writers on the history of religion, Rudolph Otto and Mircea Eliade, and again finds a paradox at work that becomes more apparent when the notion of the 'sacred space' is looked at. Taking the ancient Greek healing cult of the god Asclepius as a prototype of a sacred manifestation that is inherently therapeutic and curative, it looks at links between such an experience of the sacred and the contemporary practice of Jungian analysis, and finds that debates about the nature of transference–countertransference fall into two groups: those that make use of the notion of the sacred space as a metaphor, and those that take it literally, as founding an area of the sacred that is healing in itself, in an otherwise profane world.

JUNG AND THE AMBIVALENCE OF TRADITION

It is possible to find in Jung's writings a number of scattered pieces on the nature of tradition, and on its consequences for both the individual and the society of which they are a part.

In his autobiography, *Memories, Dreams, Reflections* (1983) Jung describes the religious doubts that confronted him as a child, and the hope that he would undergo a revelation about the nature of God at his first communion. He hoped that he would find there what his pastor father was unable to give voice to: an answer to his urgent questions, stemming from his childhood anxieties and intuitions, as to the essence of God and His relationship to humanity in general and to the individual in particular. What he found instead was a lifeless ceremony in which people did things in the 'traditionally correct manner', and in which he could see no trace of the divine mystery of incarnation, death, sacrifice and salvation that was being re-enacted (p. 71). This clash between lifeless tradition and vibrant experience was one that occupied Jung throughout his life, and that led to his interest not only in the psychology of religion, but also in the character of tradition and its relationship to the capacity for psyche wholeness – to the individuation process (see Stein 1986).

His writings touching on tradition span a period from 1912, when his *Symbols of Transformation* was published – bringing about the final painful severance between him and Freud – to 1951 when he published his work on the phenomenology of the Christ figure, *Aion*. In the earlier piece, Jung looked at the deadening effects of an over-reliance on tradition, and in the later piece, at the way in which tradition offers a way out of over-dependence on rationality or collectivity (Jung 1951: 181). In the number of writings that mention tradition between these two dates, both views are to be found, often in the same piece, making it difficult, though not impossible, to pick out a coherent argument as to the meaning and value of tradition. It becomes possible to begin such a task, when it is realized that tradition, for Jung, is not a monolithic entity: it is something that is inherently ambiguous and ambivalent. In a letter to Dr Loÿ, a fellow Swiss psychiatrist, Jung writes, in words that could be taken to be his attitude to tradition,

> I was a medical practitioner quite long enough to realize that practice obeys, and must obey, other laws than does the search for truth. One might almost say that the practitioner must submit first and foremost to the law of expediency . . . As I said to you in my last letter: 'A truth is a truth, when it works.'
>
> (Jung 1914: 264)

Jung defines tradition in various ways. It is something that is essential for the continuity of culture (1912a: 232), and for the transmission of the knowledge of our predecessors (1954b: 57); it is the distillation of great thoughts, insights and revelations, as well as being custom. It is also, however, unreflected habit – the moral and intellectual counterpart of sloth – threatening 'stagnation and cultural regression' and leading to 'a psychic regression to infantilism' and dependence (1912a: 223). As such, it is a moral problem: individuals, in Jung's view, are obliged to forge their own relationship to tradition; the refusal to confront tradition's 'hypnotic power' mesmerizes a society and keeps it 'trudging along the same old path' (1912b: 260). At the same time Jung writes of tradition as the symbolic mediator of experience too great to be grasped intellectually; this, however, has a double value as it can both save, and ruin, the soul.

This ambivalent nature of tradition is intimately entwined with the nature of psychotherapy in Jung's view; he claims that the integration of the unconscious can only be achieved along the lines already laid out by history, and will take the form of 'a new assimilation of the traditional myth'. At its most blunt, this takes the form almost of a 'payment of dues' to the past which has been neglected for historical and cultural reasons. In a 1957 interview with Richard Evans, an American professor of psychology, Jung gave an example of a young Jewish girl who had consulted him:

> Her father was a banker, and she had received an entirely worldly education. She had no idea of tradition, but then I went further into her history and found out that her grandfather had been a saddik in Galicia, and when I knew that I knew the whole story. That girl suffered from a phobia, a terrific phobia, and had already

been under psychoanalytic treatment to no effect. She was really badly plagued by that phobia, anxiety states of all sorts. And then I saw that the girl had lost the connection with her past, had lost the fact that her grandfather had been a saddik, that he lived in the myth. And her father had fallen out of it too. So I simply told her, 'You will stand up to your fear. You know what you have lost?' She didn't, of course not. I said, 'Your fear is the fear of Yahweh.' You know, the effect was that within a week she was cured after all those years of bad anxiety states, because that went through her like lightening. But I could only say that because she was absolutely lost. She thought she was in the middle of things, but she was lost, gone.

(McGuire and Hull 1980: 326)

In this example, Jung demanded a return to a relationship with a faith that was out of tune with his patient's contemporary milieu, but which was in tune with her psychological needs. The anxiety and crippling phobias that she had been experiencing were the result of her attempts to live outside of a tradition that was an integral part of herself and which demanded acknowledgement (cf. Jung 1939: 278, and Jung 1983: 160). That said, an attempt simply to copy her grandfather's mysticism would also lead to damage: the traditional myth needs to be re-experienced, re-visioned by each individual for it to meet the needs of the psyche in a 'new assimilation'.

For Jung tradition was also a social problem: societies that attempt, either intentionally or by default, to do without tradition are developmentally hazardous: they lead to barbarism and a collective prison wherever Communism prevails, and to 'spiritual regression', and 'psychic dissociation' wherever the scientific and technological materialism of the Enlightenment reigns. In these cases, just as with his Jewish patient who had become distant from a potent stream of personal revelation, an awareness of tradition prevents a collective hysteria caused by a loss of roots (Jung 1951: 181). Tradition can also, however, bind someone to mere imitation which, without the spark of individual experience can only be sterile and deadening. Caught between the demands of individual experience and the call of tradition, psychotherapy becomes not just a moral, but also a religious, problem, since the realm of the sacred needs adequate expression (1932: 341).

The disjunction between traditional opinions, inherited truths, and lived experience is, in Jung's view, the dilemma of modernity. For whatever reason, religious truths have lost their psychological validity and have become hollow; they are thus unable to sustain an individual's psychological development as the intuitions they contain are inaccessible to present day comprehension. According to Jung, the key to this process is instinct:

> The breakdown of a tradition, necessary as this may be at times, is always a loss and a danger; and it is a danger to the soul because the life of instinct – the most conservative element in man – always expresses itself in traditional usages. Age-old convictions and customs are deeply rooted in the instincts. If they get lost, the conscious mind becomes severed from its roots, while the instincts, unable to express themselves, fall back into the unconscious and reinforce its energy, causing this in turn to overflow into the existing contents of consciousness. It is then that the rootless condition of consciousness becomes a real danger.
>
> (Jung 1945a: 98)

In a sense, the symbolic language of the psyche becomes a forgotten tongue, untranslatable into contemporary experience, whose meaning can only be grasped at via the amplification of archetypal images (Jung 1945b: 273). Inner experiences of the sacred may threaten to overwhelm an individual, as there is no adequate form in which they can be contained and comprehended. The ambivalent potency of tradition is that it is able to act as a guide on the way, but also to act as a profound impediment: tradition can give rise to both salvation and to damnation. Jung's writings on the sixteenth-century Swiss physician and alchemist Paracelsus indicate the delicate balance between the two:

> The authenticity of own's own experience of nature against the authority of tradition is a basic theme of Paracelsian thinking. On this principle he based his attack on the medical schools, and his pupils carried the revolution even further by attacking Aristotelian philosophy. It was an attitude that opened the way for the scientific investigation of nature and helped to emancipate natural science from the authority of tradition. Though this liberating act had the most fruitful consequences, it also led to that conflict between knowledge and faith which poisoned the spiritual atmosphere of the nineteenth century in particular.
>
> (Jung 1942: 115)

The radical break from the past, and the privileging of a scientific, empirical rationality that characterized the Enlightenment have led to outstanding human achievements but ones that have been bought at the cost of a loss of capacity for experience of the irrational. This loss of capacity is intrinsically a dislocation within the psyche that results in anomie, neuroses and the quest for external salvation. For Jung the litmus test of tradition in these circumstances is its relationship to the individuation process and to the health of the psyche: the ability of tradition to encapsulate, and make available, psychological and spiritual truths in a way that enables an individual to make his own way through his experience, is the key. In his paper, 'Symbols of the mother and rebirth', Jung wrote (1912a: 232), 'The much vaunted ''child-likeness'' of faith only makes sense when the *feeling behind the experience is still alive*' (my italics), a view that he was to repeat when comparing religious dogma and individual experience:

> A dogma is always the result and fruit of many minds and many centuries, purified of all the oddities, shortcomings, and flaws of individual experience. But for all that, the individual experience, by its very poverty, is immediate life, the warm red blood pulsating today.
>
> (Jung 1938: 50)

The relationship between the fragility and immediacy of experience, and the familiar and profound distillations of our cultural heritage thus makes up the ambivalence within the value of tradition for Jung. It leads to the necessity of forging an individual response to manifestations of the sacred in the psyche that takes note of what has gone before, without being bound by it. Jung himself had been particularly impressed by the work of the German theologian, Rudolph Otto, whose work on sacredness is looked at below, and who he felt was able to explain much about the irresistible quality of certain psychic phenomena. As we shall see, however, Otto's work is not alone in its fruitfulness for Jungian attempts to make sense of the phenomenon of gods becoming diseases.

THE NATURE OF THE SACRED

In 1917, a German theologian and student of the phenomenology of religion, Rudolph Otto, published a book that aimed to reconcile theological thinking with religious experience. Like Jung, he had been steeped in the German Protestant tradition and had been particularly influenced by Luther and Schleiermacher, and by the philosopher Kant; in addition, he had made journeys to Greece,

Russia, Africa, and the Near and Far East to observe living religions. In his classic work, *The Idea of the Holy* (1959) he made an investigation of the character of the Holy, of the sacred, as an experience, rather than as a concept capable of rational explication and discussion. He set out to show that there is something behind the valid conceptions of God as 'spirit, reason, purpose, good will, supreme power, unity, selfhood' (p. 15), that cannot be reduced to a rational discourse, and intellectually grasped, analysed, and defined; this something is that which gives rise to these rational concepts, but which is only marginally described by them, as it is incapable of being represented in rational terms, but can only be *felt*. Otto used the Latin word *numen*, god, to coin the term 'numinous' by analogy with ominous, with which to portray the experience of the holy:

> There is only one way to help another to an understanding of it. He must be guided and led on by consideration and discussion of the matter through the ways of his own mind, until he reaches the point at which 'the numinous' perforce begins to stir, to start into life and into consciousness.
>
> (1959: 21)

This is a matter of awakening the individual spirit and so making the sacred accessible to experience, and it has its echoes in the therapeutic relationship.

In his discussion as to the qualities of the numinous, Otto outlines some of the feelings associated with it: these are feelings of confronting something which is 'wholly other' and which brings about a state that Otto describes as 'Mysterium Tremendum'. This is an emotional condition in which are mixed feelings of utter insignificance, of unutterable mystery, of awe, fascination, dread, and vitality; once experienced, it is never forgotten. For Otto, the sacred was primarily an experience, and only subsequently something that could be grasped rationally. It was, as he put it, 'the Holy as an a priori category' (p. 129). This has clear links with Jung's contention that the psyche is naturally religious, and enables him to make use of the notion of numinosity in his investigations into the relationship between an individual and the contents of the unconscious.

For the Romanian historian of religion, Mircea Eliade, on the other hand, Otto's ground-breaking formulation did not go far enough. Like Otto, Eliade had spent time investigating religious beliefs other than that of Christianity – he took his doctorate in 1933 at the University of Calcutta with an investigation into yoga – but unlike Otto, he did not ultimately privilege Christianity, preferring to investigate structures of mythological belief, and to develop a methodology for the investigation of the history of religions. He felt that Otto had attended only to the irrational character of the experience of the holy. Eliade proposed that the holy be studied as the 'sacred in its entirety' (Eliade 1961: 10), and defined the sacred as the 'opposite of the profane'. This deceptively simple definition hides an extremely subtle investigation into the relationship between the sacred and the profane, and sheds light on the nature of the sacred space. For Eliade, the sacred is a 'hierophany', a mysterious act of manifestation, of the sacred showing itself to the looker: it is

> the manifestation of something of a wholly different order, a reality that does not belong to our world, in objects that are an integral part of our natural 'profane' world.

He goes on,

> It is impossible to overemphasise the paradox represented by every hierophany, even the most elementary. By manifesting the sacred, any object becomes *something else*, yet it continues to remain *itself*, for it continues to participate in its surrounding cosmic milieu.
>
> (Eliade 1961: 11, 12)

Sacred and profane are two different, and opposed, ways of being in the world: in the one, the cosmos is sacralized and in the other, it is desacralized. For religious man, the profane cosmos is a shadow without true existence; the only thing that really exists is the area of the sacred, the 'holy ground'. Eliade indicates that this experience of the disunity of space is a primordial one, 'homologizable to the founding of the world' (p. 21), and as such enables a fundamental point of orientation to be made: the centre of a world which, up until then, had no centre, as it had no features the bounds of which could indicate any existential point, but which was homogenous and monolithic. It is only with the experience of the sacred that the universe takes on any form; without it, creation is merely a fragmented collection of different experiences of more or less indifferent spaces, driven by the spatio-temporal needs of modern living. Eliade points out that a faint trace of the experience of the uniquely orientating qualities of the hierophany can still be found in the ways in which we privilege certain places – such as our birthplace, the site of first romance, and the like – but our awareness of the subtle differences such places have to all others is a pale imitation of the differing nature of the sacred space (p. 24). The Jungian analyst, Lawrence Jaffe, indicates that childhood is particularly full of such sacralized memories:

> That is to say, there is an unacknowledged religious dimension to our experiences in childhood, and the hold our childhood has over us is due partly to the fact that in our secularised society there is nothing to take the place of the people and things and locales that childhood has sanctified.
>
> (Jaffe 1990: 45)

Psychotherapy therefore needs to investigate childhood not only to expose the beginnings of the knotting and puckering of our personalities, but also to trace our relationship to the sacred as an experience of the world (a projection) and to tease it away from our adoption of an empty tradition (an introjection). Eliade's formulation of the world-founding quality of the sacred gives a hint as to the experience of a therapeutic relationship, whereas Otto's conception of numinosity helps to explain the experience of the unconscious. The differences in implication between these two perceptions become clearer when we investigate Jungian, and post-Jungian, thinking on the process of transference–countertransference. In order to do this, however, we must first have an idea as to how the sacred space of psychotherapy may appear.

Asclepius and the sacred space of psychotherapy

The prototype of the sacred space of psychotherapy is that of the temples of the god Asclepius in ancient Greece, described by the Jungian analyst, C. A. Meier in his book, *Healing Dream and Ritual* (1989). Meier outlined the ancient Greek process of incubation – healing through a ritualized sleeping – and looked at the parallels between it and modern psychotherapy. In particular, he focused on the cult of Asclepius, the son of Apollo, who was delivered by Caesarean section as his mother, Coronis, lay dead on her funeral pyre, and raised by the great wounded healer, the centaur Chiron. True to the heroic promise of such origins, Asclepius became the pre-eminent god of healing. He accomplished his art by means of a hiero-phany within the clearly delimited therapeutic sacred space, the *temenos*, of those temples dedicated to him – the widespread Asclepieia of antiquity. The afflicted person came to the temple buildings and waited outside the sacred space until it was timely for him to enter.

When he entered, he would find a couch, lie on it and sleep, and as he slept, he would dream. Asclepius would appear to him bringing the means of healing in a manner appropriate to that individual alone. For example, at Epidaurus, there is a record of the cure of a man with crippled legs; in his dream, Asclepius appeared to him in a chariot, and after circling him three times, had the horses trample his legs (p. 25). We can here see the action of a transforming sacred space that not only conforms to the general tradition of the Asclepieia, but which also is precisely graduated to the experience of the individual supplicant.

Meier notes the complicated processes of negotiation and acceptance that occurred on the threshold of the *temenos* around the timing of the hierophany. In some cases the hierophany was indicated when the god himself appeared in a dream, or when an aspect or augery of the god was sighted; in other cases, a dream of the supplicant coincided with that of the priest, or with that of the priest's servant who could apparently dream in his stead. The threshold of the temple was thus a place of permeable boundaries. Rather than marking the limit of the sacred, it would appear the sacred bled out of the site and infused the settlements of the priests, mingling the sacred and the profane in a way which perhaps indicated the desacralization of modern times, and which allowed the growth of a properly profane medicine: that of Hippocrates, who established a form of healing rivalling that of Asclepius for centuries before triumphing (cf. Bertram 1971). In addition, it indicates that the sacred space does not only need to be geographical, but that it can also take the form of a personal experience.

What is clear about the cures of Asclepius is that without the sacred space, the hierophany could not occur. There are striking similarities between the rites and rituals associated with this ancient practice and contemporary psychotherapy: the couch, the attendants or *theraputēs*, and above all, the numinous, the active presence of something Other. Similarly, healing is affected in the same way as the original illness: in contemporary psychotherapy, the notion of working-through requires some degree of re-living the event that brought the illness with it. The petrified emotions and patterns of thought and feeling have to be delimited and described before they can come back to life again, and before meaning can return in its unique blend of the traditional and the personal.

In Asclepius we can see that it is the hierophany of the god that brings about healing at the same time that it constitutes the sacred space: it is both geographical and therapeutic, both concrete and immaterial. We can see the paradox that Eliade talked of and can begin to see the way in which the forgotten language of the psyche, the sacred, plays a part in modern psychotherapy. It does this through one of the fundamental characteristics of such therapeutic space, the curious unconscious reciprocal relationship between analyst and patient termed, in Jungian theory, transference–counter-transference, which is as much a metaphor and an actuality as the healing hierophany of Asclepius.

TRANSFERENCE–COUNTERTRANSFERENCE

In investigating the nature of transference–countertransference in Jungian theory it is advantageous to look at it in two parts: Jung's own musings on the subject, and post-Jungian thinking. This shows more clearly the way in which Jung's certainty that psychotherapy is intimately connected with experiences of the sacred, of the numinous, gives rise in post-Jungian theory to differences in the conception of the therapeutic space itself, differences that turn around the use of 'sacred space' as a metaphor, and as an actuality.

Jung's development of the notions of transference and countertransference

In 1907, on the occasion of the first meeting between C. G. Jung and Sigmund Freud, Freud suddenly asked his guest what his views were on the place of the transference in analysis. Jung was able to reply, honestly at the time, that he felt it was 'the alpha and omega of the ana-lytical method' (Jung 1946a: 172). Between 1907 and 1946, Jung's thinking on the analytic method led him to reject the Freudian analytic tradition – which he came to identify with the soulless rationality of the Enlightenment – and to adopt a tradition that had for centuries been ignored, that of medieval alchemy, the compensatory underside of an increasingly one-sided Christianity (Stein 1986). It was this that enabled him to develop the distinctive Jungian approach to the ana-lytic dialectic, a concern with the deep experience of the two people involved, and typified by the transference–countertransference. The following is a brief outline of this development (see Fordham 1974, for a fuller account).

The first conception that Jung made about the transference was that it was a bridge between an individual and reality, or rather between an individual's unconscious infantile identifications with his family, and the world in general. The process of the transference, as in the Freudian tradition, was to make the analyst the object of the patient's infantile fantasy world. This had two consequences. The first was to make the analysis of the transference essential for any successful treatment; without such analysis, the patient would simply have succeeded in co-opting the analyst into his family, and the bridge to the extra-familial world would no longer be available. The second consequence was to require that the analyst had undertaken his own personal analysis, in order to cope with the demands that the patients would make on his own infantile structures.

Jung's clinical experiences led him to supplement the Freudian view of transference. In his correspondence with Dr Loÿ, he widened its scope further to that of a social and moral entity, and a bridge to a greater maturity and 'individualization'. The transference is not only 'a projection of infantile–erotic fantasies', but is also a response to the actual character of the analyst, in an attempt via empathy and analogy, to discover the basis 'of a direct human relationship over and above merely sexual valuations' (Jung 1914: 285, 286).

Jung outlined his view of the limited role of sexual interpretations of the transference in his 1921 paper, 'The therapeutic value of abreaction'. Whilst acknowledging that interpretation of the infantile origins of neurosis is essential, the tracing of a trauma or a symptom back to its roots is not an end in itself, but rather, lays the foundations for the development of personality. Exclusively sexual interpretations of the transference act to lock the patient into an exclusively sexual relationship to the analyst, because they deny the presence in the material of the patient of the germ of his own way out of the neurosis, the 'creative element' (p. 134). The process of the transference is an attempt to have a real relationship to the analyst, one that can mediate against the dissociation that the patient is undergoing. The greater the distance between the understanding of the analyst and the psychological realities of the patient, the greater, and more sexualized, the transference. The aim of analysis becomes the aim of the transference: the removal, via analysis, of the infantile elements in the patient that mitigate against his ability to have an individual relationship, and the facing up to the problems and difficulties that then come with such a relationship. Only once this is done, can the patient realize his individuality in all the spheres of life: intellectual, moral, aesthetic, psychological and spiritual.

The move towards a sacred therapeutic space and the divergence from the Freudian tradition continued with the development of Jung's ideas on the nature of the unconscious. In *Two Essays on Analytical Psychology* (1917), Jung felt that it could be divided into a personal unconscious, and a collective or transpersonal unconsciousness. The personal unconscious corresponded roughly to Freud's conception of the unconscious, whereas the collective unconscious was the innate store of humanity's psychic heritage and potentialities, the structuring elements of which Jung termed the archetypes. This division in the unconscious was coupled with a division in the nature of transference itself: into a personal transference, made up of projections of the people important in the patient's early life – the parental and familial imagos – and an archetypal transference made up of structural elements of the patient's own personality. This archetypal transference derives from the non-subjective element of the individual, the Self, rather than the ego: Jung felt that it was activated as a consequence of the resolution of the personal transference, the analysis of projections based on infantile material. Once the energy bound up in the personal transference is released, it

> follows its own gradient down into the depths of the unconscious, and there activates what has lain slumbering from the beginning. It has discovered the hidden treasure upon which mankind ever and anon has drawn, and from which it has raised up its gods and demons, and all those potent and mighty thoughts without which man ceases to be man . . . the inherited possibilities of human imagination.
>
> (Jung 1917: 66)

The fantastical and mythical contents of the collective unconscious then become projected out in the transference. As Jung points out (p. 70), this is a time of great danger to both analyst and patient, as the contents of the projections contain not only what is best about humanity, but also what is its worst. Owing to the amount of psychic energy archetypal images contain, their action is extremely visible and powerful. Significantly, Jung likens their action on an individual to that of a religious conversion, or the onset of schizophrenia (p. 70). Unless the patient is able to distinguish these powerful projections from the actuality of the analyst, there is no way forward. Similarly, the other danger is that the patient will ascribe these numinous attributes to himself and then identify with them, seeing himself as a god.

The way out of this situation, for Jung, is to recognize the situation for what it is, and to attempt to distinguish the subjective individual from the objective, collective psyche. For this to occur, the infantile transference will have had to have been resolved, and the individual will need to be secure in whatever role and station he has in life, because 'We are here . . . confronted with the task of finding a meaning that will enable him to continue living at all – a meaning more than blank resignation and mournful retrospect' (1917: 74).

In line with Jung's conception of the psyche in general as a self-regulating system that operates in a teleological manner, so too does the archetypal transference. With the decline in the personal transference and the growth of the archetypal transference, different analytic techniques come into play: noticeably, the techniques of 'active imagination' and amplification – the exploring of the meaning of the images produced in the transference by supplementing them with the fantasies that they give rise to, and with an examination of their analogues in mythology. This involves the *translation* of images that had previously been contained in religious tradition into psychological language (Jung 1955: 226): 'that is why I take these thought-forms that have become historically fixed, try to melt them down again and pour them into moulds of immediate experience' (1938: 89), though this is no easy task.

Once the infantile transference has been resolved, and the presence of archetypal material acting in compensation for the one-sidedness of the patient's conscious life has been identified, the next task of the therapy takes place: the differentiation of 'the personal relationship to the analyst from impersonal factors' (Jung 1935: 165) – in effect the withdrawal of the archetypal projections from the analyst. This raises the question of how these activated unconscious contents can be dealt with. The answer, in line with the psychological power of the archetypal images, with *their numinosity* in Otto's term, is the development of a religious attitude, of an awareness and openness to the sacred. In this, Jung was aware of the original meaning of the term *religere* as a scrupulous observance, or careful consideration (Jung 1954a: 221); the religious attitude both endorses the experience of the sacred, and relativizes the ego. This allows the hitherto projected images to be 'contained' in Bion's sense (Bion 1963) and a *modus vivendi* reached. This enables the development within the patient of an autonomous centre of guidance, that allows the dialectic between the ego and the non-ego to continue, and so aids the development of the Self. The archetypal transference is thus, in the same way as the personal transference, an agent of psychic development, of individuation, in Jungian terms (Jung 1917: 134).

By 1946, when Jung published *The Psychology of the Transference*, his treatment of transference issues had moved away from the Freudian psychoanalytical tradition and into an alchemical sacred tradition; one of the consequences of this was an increasing interest in the analyst's emotional involvement in the analytic work, and led to examinations of countertransference issues.

The Psychology of the Transference is an extended critique of a series of ten woodcuts illustrating the 1550 alchemical text, the *Rosarium Philosophorum*, and attempts to show how the sixteenth-century alchemists were, in their attempt to transform nature and to liberate God from the grip of matter, undergoing an experience of profound psychological change and development: a maturation which Jung likens to the individuation process, and which he says the alchemists dealt with by projecting their psychological processes into the matter they were working with. It is for this reason that Jung considers the alchemists as true forerunners of modern psychotherapists, and feels able to draw on the woodcuts to illustrate the nature of the archetypal transference. The woodcuts show a process of relationship, death and rebirth, indicated by the progressive transformation of a royal couple, a King and Queen into a winged hermaphroditic creature that signifies the transcendence of opposites. Jung takes these opposites to be not just male and female but also self and other, and sees the gradual effects of the alchemical process as an overcoming of projections, as an operation of a mutual relationship between analyst and patient through the play of an increasingly numinous transference–countertransference.

The first woodcut sets the scene, and the second (Figure 1) shows the beginning of the relationship of the King and Queen. Jung comments that whilst the picture is about human love, it also has overtones of incest, stemming from an allusion to the brother and sister, Apollo and Diana; it is the intercession of the Holy Ghost that lifts the incest to a spiritual realm. It thus becomes part of the motif of individuation: 'Incest symbolises union with one's own being, it means individuation or becoming a self' (1946a: 218).

For Jung, this is a description of the personal, infantile transference, in which the analyst becomes a part of the pattern of family relating, as a result of the projection of infantile fantasies previously held by other members of the family – mother, father, brother, or sister. At the same time, however, the personality of the analyst is deeply involved in this process, and Jung indicates the complexity of this involvement by pointing out that in the analysis, as in

Figure 1   Originally form *Rosarium Philosophorum*, published Frankfurt, 1550; Figure 2 in C. J. Jung (1946) *The Practice of Psychotherapy*, CW 16: 213.

the situation of the King and Queen, there is a six-way relationship going on:

    between the analyst and his unconscious;
    between the patient and his unconscious;
    between the analyst and patient as conscious individuals;
    between the unconscious of the analyst and patient;
    between the consciousness of the analyst and the unconscious of the patient;
    between the consciousness of the patient and the unconscious of the analyst.

It is here that issues of countertransference begin to be more clearly formulated.

Commenting on the phenomenon that the transference 'divides quite as much as it connects' (1946a: 233), Jung puts forward the idea that the transference contains within itself an instinctual element of 'kinship libido', the desire for a real human connection. Individuation has thus a double aspect: a subjective process of fruition, and an objective process of relationship to others. Jung comments that an unbalanced assumption of either one is a danger to the individual and to the group, noting that an unmediated acceptance of the kinship libido at the social level, as opposed to the psychological, leads to a mass psychology, and totalitarian regimes. Working with the transference is thus working in an area 'but lately visited by the numen, where the whole weight of mankind's problems has settled' (p. 235).

The stripping away of infantile projections indicated by the second picture of the *Rosarium* has begun the process of transformation, and what lies behind the everyday appearance is now revealed. For Jung this is the shadow, those aspects of the whole personality that are unacceptable to the individual, or incompatible with his conception of himself, but which need to be acknowledged and integrated with the ego to the extent that this is possible. The attempt to regain those aspects of the personality that remain projected on to others continues, and the process becomes increasingly unconscious. Jung comments that it is at this stage in the analysis of the transference that the process appears to become stuck: in theory both the analyst and the patient now know enough for the transference to have been 'dissolved away', yet it remains there in full force. Jung's view is that both parties do better by waiting and seeing what kind of a birth will result from the union, giving up their attempts at control, and keeping in mind their limitations, for, 'not everything can and must be cured' (p. 254). It is at this point that Jung's alchemical outline leaves psychoanalytic notions of transference behind and enters into the sacred space of Jungian analysis.

In the woodcuts, this is represented by an image of the King and Queen joined together in one body and, at this stage, lifeless (Figure 2). This death is the death of the ego, and is also the point at which mere tradition fails the individual. The withdrawal of the vast number of projections that the individual has made on other people, together with the acceptance of the shadow, means that the ego is already highly relativized; this is taken further by the tendency of the individual to identify with some of the psychic contents awaiting integration – resulting in an 'inflation' of the personality in a

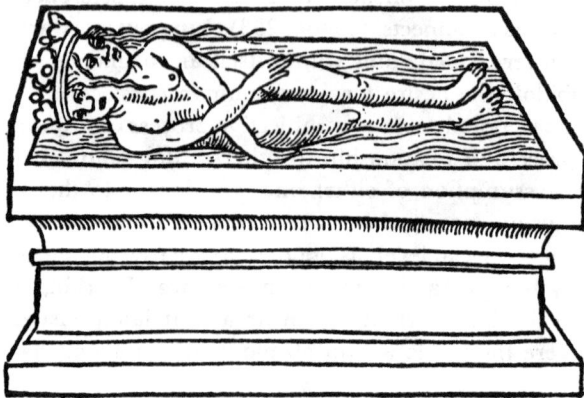

Figure 2 Originally from *Rosarium Philosophorum*, published Frankfurt, 1550; Figure 6 in C. J. Jung (1946) *The Practice of Psychotherapy*, CW 16: 259.

way that can alternate between a form of megalomania and a deep depersonalization. The new birth is not yet ready, and further decay has yet to occur.

This is a time of great disorientation and dissociation for the patient, as existing ego-consciousness is in a state of collapse. Jung comments on the hazardousness of this state:

> It is closely analogous to the schizophrenic state, and it should be taken very seriously because this is the moment when latent psychoses may become acute, i.e., when the patient becomes aware of the collective unconscious and the psychic non-ego.
>
> (1946a: 267)

The role of the analyst in this state is to act as a point of orientation for the patient, to use his own experience of this state to enable the patient to make sense of what is happening to him, for it is the understanding of the experience that enables the patient to begin to emerge out of it, with a perspective made up of both conscious and unconscious.

Gradually there is a return of a relationship between ego and unconscious, an inner relationship that is predicated on an outer relationship between analyst and patient. This relationship is not, however, an easy one; even though the ego has been discriminated from the unconscious, the unconscious still has to be reckoned with. A balance has to be drawn between the demands of the ego and the world, and those of the unconscious and the inner life; between tradition and experience. It is the holding of this difficult balance that brings about the new birth.

Figure 3 Originally from *Rosarium Philosophorum*, published Frankfurt, 1550; Figure 10 in C. J. Jung (1946) *The Practice of Psychotherapy*, CW 16: 307.

The final picture in the *Rosarium* shows the triumphal scene of the new birth of the winged hermaphrodite (Figure 3). This is the goal of the alchemists, the 'philosophical stone', by which everything can be transmuted. The inorganic, organic, animal and spiritual worlds have now been combined in one figure, which is, paradoxically, its own creator: the process of the integration of consciousness and the unconscious brings about the element in the psyche without which the process is impossible. For Jung, it is the existence of this paradox that

> offers the possibility of an *intuitive* and *emotional* experience, because the unity of the self, unknowable and incomprehensible, irradiates even the sphere of our discriminating, and hence, divided, consciousness, and, like all unconscious contents, does so with very powerful effects.
>
> (1946a: 314)

Jung's discussion of the final picture, of its monstrous nature and its dependence on an explicit sexual template gives rise to his comment that it indicates why the alchemists failed in their task: their consciousness had not advanced beyond an instinctual sexuality, so that the union of supreme opposites could do no more than result in a hybrid figure. He comments pointedly that the images that the alchemists used to describe their work were the same images that gripped Freud when he developed his psychology in a later, scientific age:

> The problem of the union of opposites had been lying there for centuries in its sexual form, yet it had to wait until scientific enlightenment and objectivity had advanced far enough for people to mention 'sexuality' in scientific conversation . . . The natural archetypes that underlie the mythologems of incest, the *hieros gamos* [sacred marriage], the divine child etc., blossomed forth – in the age of science – into the theory of infantile sexuality, perversions, and incest, while the *coniunctio* was rediscovered in the transference neurosis.
>
> (1946a: 317–18)

The basic problem, underlying both alchemical and psychoanalytic theories, and by default his own, was the question of understanding, responding to and perhaps abolishing, 'the profound cleavage in man and the world' (p. 318): the breach between God and humanity, good and evil, matter and spirit, tradition and experience. He felt that the best hope of solving the problem was by the process outlined by the alchemists in the *Rosarium Philosophorum*: the process of the gradual withdrawal of projections from others, and the integration of consciousness and the unconscious by the unfolding of a centredness that took account of both – the Self – through the development of the religious attitude. The phenomenon of transference–countertransference is thus of 'central significance . . . in psychotherapy on the one hand and in the field of normal human relationships on the other' (p. 321).

It is clear from this outline of the development of Jung's notions of transference and countertransference that Jung's conception of analytic space is that of a dynamic dialectical relationship between analyst and patient; in other words, that for the patient's transference there is a corresponding countertransference, and that this is a usual and expected part of the therapeutic relationship. Jung's stress on the personal involvement of the therapist in the analysis was in sharp contrast to the approach held towards countertransference by Freud and the early Freudians. The psychoanalyst Margaret Little has remarked that in the early days of psychoanalysis, the occasion of an analyst dreaming about a patient was treated as a sign that the analyst not only needed more analysis, but that he should also hand the patient over to someone else (Little 1986: 281). Jung would have found such an attitude ridiculous because of his conviction that the analyst is as much *in* the analysis as the patient, the difference being one of degree rather than kind. Both are required to face the experience of the numinous, and to wrestle with the task of integrating the sacred into the personality. This task is both unique for each individual, and yet ancient and commonplace.

Post-Jungian conceptions of transference–countertransference

In the same way that Jung's works have given rise to a large number of different, even contradictory, interpretations and uses (Stein 1986: 2), so too do Jungian analysts after Jung have differing views of the value of transference–countertransference as a therapeutic tool. These post-Jungian debates focus on issues of technique in psychotherapy which are themselves based on the ambivalence of the therapeutic sacred space: the irrational numinous area of the experience of the unconscious indicated by Otto, and the paradoxical world-founding and transcending quality of the sacred identified by Eliade. These debates can be seen as turning around two differing conceptions of sacred space: the one, as a metaphor of the analytic process – one which helps explain it more clearly and is of heuristic value; and the other, as an experience that is concrete and literal, in which the play of transference–countertransference between the analyst and patient founds an arena of the gods, a healing and transforming *temenos*.

Sacred space as metaphor

The 'as if' quality of metaphor enables it to illuminate areas of life that may otherwise have remained murky, without intending to describe those areas exactly. Thus, in terms of the analytic relationship, the metaphor 'sacred space' indicates first, the strange, unsocial quality of analysis, its eschewment of the customary social norms of dialogue and interaction, and the fact that one of the parties generally has to pay the other to behave towards him in such a way; second, it indicates that this relationship is a special one, over and above its strangeness, that it is protected by its guaranteed time, its freedom from interruption, and the open-endedness of the commitment; third, it indicates that there is a result of this curious relationship, that something will happen as a result of both the technique and setting, a transformation of an individual by the process of analysis, in a way which will not only free him of his infantile conflicts, but which will also enable a flexibility of relationship to the personally experienced sacred (cf. Siegelman 1990).

In this version of Jungian analysis, typified by the work of the so-called 'London' or 'Developmental' school (Fordham 1978, Samuels 1985), transference–countertransference has a vital role. In this, it has received stimulus from developments in psychoanalysis after Freud, particularly from the work of Klein, Winnicott, Racker and Searles, though it has retained its characteristic 'Jungian feel', and its engagement with the numinous world of the archetypal image. 'Countertransference' in some views becomes extended in its scope to include all the non-neurotic, non-psychopathological reactions that the analyst may have towards the patient, both conscious, and unconscious; both within the session, and outside it. In this, it is a reflection of the whole personality of the analyst, including the personal factors that influenced his choice of profession, and concerns itself with the relationship as a whole between the analyst and patient. The interaction between the analyst and the patient brings about a transformative field that has its roots in a shared unconscious relationship structured by archetypal material: Jung's *participation mystique*, or Winnicott's metaphorical or potential space (Winnicott 1951).

Work on the nature of the analyst's countertransference reactions has tended to make a distinction between those which are more clearly conscious, and those which are either on the threshold of consciousness, or unconscious, and which tend therefore to be conceived of in terms of the psychic mechanisms of projection, introjection and projective identification. Fordham (1957) identified two types of countertransference: *illusory* and *syntonic*. Illusory countertransference comes about when the material of the patient activates an unresolved area of the analyst's own experience, past or present, in such a way that the patient becomes obscured behind the eruption of the analyst's material. Analysis becomes impossible until the analyst recognizes what is happening, and deals with it appropriately. Syntonic countertransference, on the other hand, comes about when the analyst registers that an emotional state he is experiencing is the result of a projection of the patient's material; in other words, when the analyst experiences the patient's unconscious within himself, and is then able to use these experiences as the material for interpretation (see also Fordham 1969). As Fordham puts it, 'It can be just as valid for the analyst to know of the projection through registering its impact upon himself, as it is by listening to the patient and realizing it as an inference from what the patient says' (Fordham 1957: 145). The difference between these two types of countertransference is not always easy to discover, however, given the mutual relations of patient and analyst. In some senses, the disputes amongst Jungian analysts over the definition and importance of transference and countertransference are disputes over the nature of analytic work. Transference–countertransference issues are highlighted where emphasis is given to technique and clinical work, and played down where emphasis is given to the art of analysis, with its concomitant stress on symbol interpretation and on the free play and exploration of archetypal images (Machtiger 1985: 91). The former tends to be found more in work that concentrates on freeing the individual from his past, whilst the latter tends to be found more in work that concentrates on aiding an individual's quest for wholeness. It is the latter emphasis that serves to privilege the reality of the sacred space.

Sacred space as actuality

Eliade's view of the world-founding quality of the sacred is the other sense in which the term 'sacred space' has been taken to apply to Jungian analytic work. This is a literal description, not a metaphorical one. Though the obvious features of the analytic setting remain the same, the difference is that for some Jungians the setting of the analysis and the analytic relationship that comes from it results in a rending of the secular world and the emergence of a potent,

transfiguring arena of the sacred which itself brings about transformation.

In this view, Jungian analysts emphasize the archetypal transference, as it is felt that it carries with it aspects of the whole personality
that are unconscious and unrealized, and is an archetypal blueprint,
as it were, of the individuation process and the development of the
Self. This has tended to be dealt with by edification: the amplification
of the transference images and themes in terms of their previous
incarnations in the cultural and religious history of mankind. The
'gods behind the disease' are recognized for what they are, and the
patient develops into a *homo religious*, a change in attitude that reduces
the importance of the ego, and allows the development of the Self as
the centre and circumference of the personality.

This, rather than any great claims for a narrow therapeutic
effectiveness – the cure of symptoms – is a characteristic feature of
Jungian analysis. Adolf Guggenbühl-Craig, a Jungian based in
Zurich, commented on the similar effectiveness of various forms of
psychotherapy, and on the charge that one form of psychotherapy is
therefore as good as any other. In a way which is characteristic of this
sensitivity to the sacred he pointed out that it was the ritualistic
character of regular attendance at Jungian therapy that brought
about the healing, rather than the style of therapy itself. In this sense,
he commented, confession and analytical psychology have much in
common (Guggenbühl-Craig 1972).

A more dynamic variant of this can be seen in Steinberg's discussion of the nature of the therapeutic relationship, where he
indicates that, just as it is their experience of being a 'wounded
healer' that causes people to become analysts, so too is it this
experience that works therapeutically with their patients:

> Being wounded is not just an inevitable and painful fate, it is also a
> necessary aspect of helping others. It is only through the knowledge
> derived from attempting to heal one's own wounds that the therapist
> can help others. In addition, the therapist does not heal the other
> directly, but by arousing the healing process in the patient's
> unconscious. The analyst serves as a model of a healed person.
> This constellates the wounded healer archetype in the patient's
> unconscious, and that actually does the healing, not the analyst.
> (Steinberg 1990: 27–8)

Steinberg indicates that though the differences between the personal
and the archetypal transferences are not always easy to perceive,

there is a difference in how they are experienced. With archetypal material, its inherent numinosity brings about a condition of exaggerated feeling over and beyond any exaggeration brought about by more mundane material. Asclepius can be seen more clearly in this conception of psychotherapy: the analyst as the servant of the god maintains the sanctity of the *temenos* and prepares the supplicant for his meeting with the god, the Other in themselves; a meeting which lasts over years and which has the atmosphere of a shared entry into the sacred.

There is, however, a further view that has resulted from this concrete experience of the sacred. This is the view that Jung's work is not just a psychology of religion – an examination of religious sensibility – but is itself a 'psychotherapy of a religious tradition' (Stein 1986), a healing of the God-image of the Judeo-Christian heritage. In the numinous contents of the archetypal unconscious we find, not merely a realm of the sacred, but God Himself, in so far as we are capable of experiencing Him. In this view, Jungian analysis, in ensuring the development of the Self, also enables the development of God through His continued incarnation in humanity (Dourley 1984, Edinger 1987 and Jaffe 1990).

IN CONCLUSION: JUNGIAN TRADITION AND IMMEDIATE EXPERIENCE

Ulanov points out that in spite of the difference in the conception of transference–countertransference held by different schools of Jungian analysts, there are two basic areas of agreement (Ulanov 1985). The first is that each transference–countertransference relationship is a unique one; the second is that transference–countertransference operates on different levels, and that the distinctive contribution of Jungians to its investigation is the emphasis on its archetypal qualities. Transference–countertransference phenomena are seen as stemming not only from infantile conflicts, objective reactions and unconscious communications, but also from the archetype-driven process of individuation that requires an 'Other' to come to fruition (Jung 1946a). Likewise, Jacoby (1984) emphasizes that the transference always has its archetypal roots, and that these are constructed around instinctual needs and the fantasies related to them. As a consequence, when the transference comes to be interpreted, the analyst not only looks towards the infantile conflicts that it expresses but also asks the question, 'What does it mean for the psychic healing process that a particular kind of transference is produced by the unconscious in the specific analytic situation?' (p. 83). In other words, what is the purpose and goal of the transference? A balance between the attractions of the amplification and elucidation of archetypal symbols and their links to ancient mythology, and the detective-like investigation of the patterns of infantile object-relating thus needs to be drawn, if the patient is to be enabled to come to terms both with his past and with his future.

Barbara Stevens Sullivan (1989) has examined the experiential structure of psychotherapy by looking at its parallels with the structures of the universal hero myth, with patterns of symbolic healing, and with work on the pattern of feminine development within analysis. She shows how 'symbolic healing', the attempt to explain or to provide a context for an individual's suffering, as opposed to 'scientific healing', the attempt to provide a concrete cure for a malady, underlies analytic work, particularly Jungian work with its emphasis on 'wholeness' rather than 'cure', and indicates that the structure of analytic work has clear parallels with both mythological themes and primitive processes of healing.

It is this that leads Jungians to assert not only the existence of archetypal material within the analytic session, and the archetypally-grounded development of the personality, but also that the very setting and process of analysis and psychotherapy have an archetypal foundation. The processes of projection, introjection, projective identification, resistance, transference and countertransference become more than technical difficulties, but are also experiences of the sacred in the heart of the process of healing. Western religious traditions, no longer able to manifest the hierophany of the numinous in ways that meet the reality of inner experience, need therefore to be translated to fulfil the needs of modernity.

Does this mean that Jungian theory and practice, in its attempt to fulfil these needs, can now be said to make up a tradition of its own? Given the ambivalent nature of tradition in general and the differing ways that it can act to inhibit and to encourage individual development, this is not a simple question. Jung's comments in a letter of 1946 to J. H. van der Hoop give some kind of an answer:

> I can only hope and wish that no one becomes 'Jungian'. I stand for no doctrine, but describe facts and put forward certain views which I hold worthy of discussion . . . I leave everyone free to deal with the facts in his own way, since I also claim this freedom for myself.
> (Jung 1946b: 405)

Debates about the nature of transference–countertransference, about the experience of the psyche in the realm of the sacred, are unfinished in Jungian thought because they rely on this irresolvable tension between tradition and experience. As much as Jungian thinking succeeds in distilling truth from its investigations into the psyche and into the process of gods becoming diseases, it will always fall short: the tradition that it becomes will be able to illuminate the lives of those who come after it, but their individual realization of the psyche, of the sacred within themselves and within the *temenos* of the analytic space, and of the ebb and flow of transference–countertransference, will always demand that any such truth as may be found be melted down again and poured into the fragile, living moulds of immediate experience.

ACKNOWLEDGEMENT

The author would like to thank Edward Herst and, especially, Golshad Ghiaci for their encouragement, support and patience during the writing of this chapter.

REFERENCES

Bertram, G. (1971) 'Hippocrates – an archetypal image of the individuation way of the physician', in J. Wheelwright (ed.) *The Analytic Process: Aims, Analysis, Training*, New York: G. P. Putman's Sons.

Bion, W. R. (1963) *Elements of Psychoanalysis*, London: Heinemann.

Dourley, J. P. (1984) *The Illness That We Are: a Jungian Critique of Christianity*, Toronto: Inner City Books.

Edinger, E. F. (1987) *The Christian Archetype: a Jungian Commentary on the Life of Christ*, Toronto: Inner City Books.

Eliade, M. (1961) *The Sacred and the Profane: the Nature of Religion*, New York and Evanston: Harper & Row.

Fordham, M. (1957) 'Notes on the transference', in M. Fordham, R. Gordon, J. Hubback and K. Lambert (eds) (1989) *Technique in Jungian Analysis*, London: Karnac Books.

—— (1969) 'Technique and counter-transference', in M. Fordham, R. Gordon, J. Hubback and K. Lambert (eds) (1989) *Technique in Jungian Analysis*, London: Karnac Books.

—— (1974) 'Jung's concept of transference', *Journal of Analytical Psychology* 19(1): 1.

—— (1978) *Jungian Psychotherapy: a Study in Analytical Psychology*, Chichester: John Wiley & Sons.

Guggenbühl-Craig, A. (1972) 'Analytical rigidity and ritual', *Spring* 1972: 34–42.

Jacoby, M. (1984) *The Analytic Encounter: Transference and Human Relationships*, Toronto: Inner City Books.

Jaffe, L. W. (1990) *Liberating the Heart: Spirituality and Jungian Psychology*, Toronto: Inner City Books.

Jung, C. G. (1912a) 'Symbols of transformation', in *Symbols of Transformation*, C. G. Jung, *Collected Works*, London: Routledge & Kegan Paul (CW) 5.

—— (1912b) 'New paths in psychology', in *Two Essays on Analytical Psychology*, CW 7.

—— (1914) 'Some crucial points in psychoanalysis: a correspondence between Dr. Jung and Dr. Loÿ', in *Freud and Psychoanalysis*, CW 4.

—— (1917) 'On the psychology of the unconscious', in *Two Essays on Analytical Psychology*, CW 7.

—— (1921) 'The therapeutic value of abreaction', in *The Practice of Psychotherapy*, CW 16.

—— (1932) 'Psychotherapists or the clergy', in *Psychology and Religion*, CW 11.

—— (1935) 'The Tavistock lectures', in *The Symbolic Life*, CW 18.

—— (1938) 'Psychology and religion, the Terry Lectures', in *Psychology and Religion*, CW 11.

—— (1939) 'The symbolic life', in *The Symbolic Life*, CW 18.

—— (1942) 'Paracelsus as a spiritual phenomenon', in *Alchemical Studies*, CW 13.

—— (1945a) 'Psychotherapy today', in *The Practice of Psychotherapy*, CW 16.

—— (1945b) 'The philosophical tree', in *Alchemical Studies*, CW 13.

—— (1946a) 'Psychology of the transference', in *The Practice of Psychotherapy*, CW 16.

—— (1946b) 'Letter to J. H. van der Hoop', in G. Adler (ed.) (1973) *C. G. Jung: Letters*, vol. 1, London: Routledge & Kegan Paul.

—— (1951) 'Aion', in *Aion: Researches into the Phenomenology of the Self*, CW 9(ii).

—— (1954a) 'On the nature of the psyche', in *The Structure and Dynamics of the Psyche*, CW 8.

—— (1954b) 'Concerning the Archetypes, with special reference to the anima concept', in *The Archetypes and the Collective Unconscious*, CW 9(i).

—— (1955) 'Letter to Pater Lucas Menz', in G. Adler (ed.) (1975) *C. G. Jung: Letters*, vol. 2. Princeton, NJ: Princeton University Press.

—— (1957) 'The secret of the golden flower', in *Alchemical Studies*, CW 13.

—— (1983) *Memories, Dreams, Reflections*, London: Fontana.

Little, M. (1986) *Transference Neurosis and Transference Psychosis: Towards Basic Unity*, London: Free Association Books and Maresfield Library.

Machtiger, H. G. (1985) 'Countertransference/Transference', in M. Stein (ed.) *Jungian Analysis*, Boston: Shambhala.

McGuire, W. and Hull, R. F. C. (1980) *C. G. Jung Speaking: Interviews and Encounters*, London: Picador.

Meier, C. A. (1989) *Healing Dream and Ritual: Ancient Incubation and Modern Psychotherapy*, Einsiedeln: Daimon Verlag.

Otto, R. (1959) *The Idea of the Holy*, Harmondsworth: Penguin Books.

Samuels, A. (1985) *Jung and the Post-Jungians*, London: Routledge & Kegan Paul.

Siegelman, E. M. (1990) 'Metaphors of the therapeutic encounter', *Journal of Analytical Psychology*, vol. 35(2): 175–92.

Stein, M. (1986) *Jung's Treatment of Christianity: the Psychotherapy of a Religious Tradition*, Wilmette, Ill.: Chiron Publications.

Steinberg, W. (1990) *Circles of Care: Clinical Issues in Jungian Therapy*, Toronto: Inner City Books.

Sullivan, B. Stevens (1989) *Psychotherapy Grounded in the Feminine Principle*, Wilmette, Ill.: Chiron Publications.

Ulanov, A. B. (1985) 'Transference/countertransference: a Jungian perspective', in M. Stein (ed.) *Jungian Analysis*, Boston: Shambhala.

Winnicott, D. W. (1951) 'Transitional objects and transitional phenomena', in *Through Paediatrics to Psycho-analysis*, London: Hogarth Press.

Chapter 4

D. W. Winnicott and a personal tradition

Nina Farhi

Donald Winnicott was the embodiment of a particularly English philosophic disposition which valued both the empirical and scientific. At the same time it espoused the romantic tradition, with its emphasis on freedom and spontaneity of conception and expression.

In the 1940s and the 1950s the ideological conflicts in the British Psycho-Analytical Society between two major immigrant cultural figures, Anna Freud and Melanie Klein, sought to establish a kind of primacy. Winnicott, however, steeped in the more confident tradition of the English nonconformist West Country, could disclaim any intention of setting about his work with an academic's sensibility to intellectual hierarchies. He was uninterested in the intricacies of carefully mapping sources and developments in such a way that would demonstrate the inevitability of his particular point of departure.

He introduces his influential paper, 'Primitive emotional development', first published in 1945, with characteristic flourish:

> I shall not first give an historical survey and show the development of my ideas from the theories of others, because my mind does not work that way. What happens is that I gather this and that, here and there, settle down to clinical experience, form my own theories and then, last of all, interest myself in looking to see where I stole what. Perhaps this is as good a method as any.
>
> (Winnicott 1982a: 145. All subsequent references are to Winnicott unless otherwise indicated.)

He recognized in later life that he had irritated many colleagues by this disregard of his antecedents and endeavoured to make slight amends in a personal piece he gave in 1967 to the grouping of independent psychoanalysts called the 1952 Club. He acknowledged that at heart his creativity was enlivened by a quite different process, a process that is epitomized in his major psychoanalytic contribution, his theory of playing (1989: 573).

Masud Khan, that astute poet of human nature, wrote of Winnicott that it became

> progressively more important [for him] to define the role of imagination, illusion and playing in the transitional area and space from which all true spontaneous gestures of self-actualization are initiated and crystallised into a *personal tradition* [my italics] of inner reality, which is more than fantasying.
>
> (Khan 1982: xvi)

By pursuing the two threads of playing and tradition, and especially the meaning of Khan's potent phrase, 'a personal tradition', this chapter seeks to examine Winnicott's peculiarly English approach both to theory-building and to creativity in general.

THE LOCATION OF A PERSONAL TRADITION

Winnicott's passionate letter to Melanie Klein in November 1952 arose out of his deep disquiet at the stranglehold he believed Klein's followers were putting round the psychoanalytic body; in it he asserts more than his personal pain at his curious exclusion from Mrs Klein's gifted circle (1987: 33–7). This accusation is central to his whole understanding of a question that he, as a psychoanalyst, was perhaps alone in asking.

'What is life about?', he asks in *Playing and Reality* (1971). For him the answer lay in creating for oneself a 'personal tradition', as Masud Khan described it, in the ordinary world ready to be found. Furthermore, Winnicott was pointing to the vital difference between 'what the world offered' and 'what the individual created'. In this difference, where consciousness of space and time dissolved, resided the potentiality of the individual's creativity. It is in this potential space, 'the third area', as Winnicott called it, where the human being attained his individuality, his sense of being, of being real, and his sense of uniqueness, that the truly personal tradition was to be found.

Even so, Winnicott, like his contemporary Marion Milner, attributed to the artist, in whatever field, and to the individually created life, only a temporary resolution in the struggle to capture the moment of illusion. This is the point at which an identity seems possible between what is in the world and what is created by the individual out of need. Such an identity goes hand in hand with the vital illusion that it is indeed possible to communicate deeply and directly in shared experience. In Marion Milner's words, 'to believe in the full reality of the *other*', is itself a creative achievement almost without parallel. Such moments, which Winnicott located in the whole cultural field, were however only temporary resting places, a solace in the constant struggle of allaying the fundamental isolation of individual existence. But they were, both for Winnicott and Milner, the very stuff of creative life. In Milner's words, these were the moments when 'the original poet in each one of us created the outside world for us, by finding the familiar in the unfamiliar' (Milner 1971).

This, too, is Berenson's 'aesthetic moment' in visual art, quoted by Milner in her 1952 paper, 'The role of illusion in symbol formation'. Berenson writes,

In visual art the aesthetic moment is that fleeting instant, so brief as to be almost timeless, when the spectator is at one with the work of art he is looking at, or with actuality of any kind that the spectator sees in terms of art, as form and colour. He ceases to be his ordinary self, and the picture or building, statue, landscape, or aesthetic actuality is no longer outside himself. The two become one entity. Time and space are abolished and the spectator is possessed by one awareness. When he recovers workaday consciousness it is as if he had been initiated into illuminating formative mysteries.

(Milner 1952: 97)

Milner and Winnicott, as well as Christopher Bollas (1987: 28) more recently, make claims for the aesthetic moment outside the area of art itself, in the everyday experience of the healthy infant and adult.

Winnicott disagreed with Klein's followers precisely because he questioned whether a truth could be discovered, announced as finally achieved and then just left to sustain all future generations. He protested to Klein that her follower, Joan Riviere, was suggesting that Klein had indeed laid out a kind of complete jigsaw of the psyche; that all the pieces were now clearly in view and that 'further work will only consist in the fitting together of the pieces' (1987: 35).

We may understand the vehemence of Winnicott's statement when he wrote to Klein,

I personally think that it is very important that your work should be restated by people discovering in their own way and presenting what they discover in their own language. It is only in this way that the language will be kept alive. If you make the stipulation that in future only your language shall be used for the statement of other people's discoveries then the language becomes a dead language.

(1987: 35)

And when Winnicott goes on to say to Klein, 'Your ideas will only live in so far as they are rediscovered and reformulated by original people in the psychoanalytic movement and outside it' (ibid.), we can understand that he is laying siege to something greater than a dispute over language; the battleground was not just the narrow one of personal animosity.

For Winnicott then, there was, as Masud Khan claims for Goethe, a personal need for a 'quickening in . . . activity', in order to bring to life personal discovery and personal meaning; it would be brought about by something far greater than the handing down of given knowledge. As Khan suggests, Winnicott 'could learn from others only if it awakened him more sharply and largely towards his own self' (Khan 1982: xvi). In Winnicott's language it is this 'creative apperception more than anything else that makes life worth living' (Winnicott 1971: 76). By this he surely means that what comes to have personal meaning can only become so through contact with what Winnicott came to call the 'self-created world'.

In a letter to Roger Money-Kyrle which he wrote in the same month as the letter to Melanie Klein, already quoted, he lays this thesis bare:

I think we must take it for granted that emotionally there is no contribution from the individual to the environment or from the environment to the individual. The individual only communicates with a self-created world and the people in the environment only communicate with the individual in so far as they can create him or her . . . Nevertheless, in health there is the illusion of contact and it is this which provides the high spots of human life and which makes the arts among the most important of human experience.

(1987: 43)

Perhaps in a more generous spirit, Marion Milner captures the recurrence of such moments in our lives that, to some extent, attenuate Winnicott's concept of the individual as an isolate, 'permanently non-communicating, permanently unknown, in fact unfound'. She writes, what did it mean if these ideals which are *significant*, perpetual and as constant as the nature which expresses them really are our dreams? What did it mean if these spirits in our pantheon which, temporarily or permanently, find resting places in the outer world of persons or places or things, what did it mean if they are really our dreams, really the inner created pictures of what we love most in the world, pictures of what we hunger for? Did it mean that though it was an illusion when one thinks one has found the exact embodiment of that goodness in the external world, since outer reality is never the same as our dreams, yet such moments are the vital illusions by which we live? Did it mean that they are the actual moments when the forms of imagination do happily grow significant and without which, somewhere in our lives, we should have no drive to seek permanent objectives in the external world, without which we should only be driven by blind instinct and animal appetite? Did it mean that they are moments in which one does not have to decide which is one self and which is the other – *moments of illusion, but illusions that are perhaps the essential root* of a high morale and vital enthusiasm for living – moments which can perhaps be most often experienced in physical love combined with in-loveness, but also which need not always require bodily contact and physical sexual experience but which can be imaginatively experienced in an infinite variety of contacts with the world?

(Milner 1971: 29)

In Winnicott's concept of illusion too there is a vitally important development from that of Freud. Freud's emphasis on illusion as forming the bulwark against the infant's apprehension of the reality principle fitted well within the spirit of nineteenth-century rationalism and objectivity. For Freud, illusion contained the notion of deceit. Winnicott as well as Marion Milner were, however, centrally preoccupied precisely with the internal relationship, the play between that which was perceived and that which was apperceived. Illusion, in their vocabulary, thus came to have the meaning of that which was in play (*in-ludere*), the enrichment of an engagement with the world, not at all a defence against anxiety brought about by the world.

Milner, using Berenson's concept of the 'aesthetic moment' conveys this enrichment to living that flows from the very surrendering of the discriminating ego subjected to the reality principle. She gives to play, as Winnicott did, the transforming capacity of relating inner to outer and of infinitely enhancing the quality of life through the blurring of boundaries (Milner 1987: 98). Similarly, Winnicott de-scribed the area of illusion, fostered by the mother's adaptive presence, as the formative experience that allowed an infant to develop a relationship with external reality, even to discover reality itself, and thence onwards in a continuous dialectical movement between inner and outer psychic reality. 'It is not possible', Winnicott claimed, 'for the infant to begin to develop a capacity to experience a relationship to external reality or even to form a conception of reality', without experiencing the illusion of omnipotence (1982a: 238).

For Winnicott, Freud's concept of the pleasure principle as it con-flicted with the reality principle was insufficient for explaining an infant's psychic development. Nevertheless, in the evolution of his theory of the transitional area, the potential space between inner and outer reality, it is possible to see Winnicott's use of Freud's earlier conceptions, to fashion his radically creative and transformative unfolding: his originality based on an established tradition.

It is not hard, then, to discern the fundamental antagonism that lies between the almost perfect and complete construction of the psyche that Joan Riviere inferred in the theoretical work of Melanie Klein, and that which Winnicott and Milner understood as the creative process, including the process of theory-building. For Winnicott, it was this 'creative apperception' more than anything else that made for a sense of aliveness. For him, it was necessary to fight all the time to feel creative, to feel real, to feel alive. And, for Winnicott, to be alive was all. Acceptance of theory as given for all time would have carried with it the notion of compliance; and compliance, for Winnicott, spelled futility for the individual, as if, in his words in *Playing and Reality*, the individual were to have become 'caught up in the creativity of someone else, or of a machine' (1971: 76).

PLAYING AND PSYCHOANALYSIS

In *Playing and Reality*, Winnicott's fullest and most mature exposition of his conceptualization of creativity and playing, he seeks to redraw the sequence that placed play within the limited context of psycho-analysis. Whilst deeply admiring Klein's innovative use of play material in analytic sessions, he wished to look at psychoanalysis itself as a sophisticated form of playing. 'Psychotherapy takes place in the overlap of two areas of playing, that of the patient and that of the therapist. Psychotherapy has to do with two people playing together'

(1971: 44). Thus, although playing was a form of communication that took place within the specialized setting of the analytic hour, in itself it was a universal phenomenon long predating its twentieth-century aspect. Although it is to Klein that psychoanalysis turns for a consideration of play content, it is in Winnicott's formulations that playing 'as a thing in itself' comes to the fore. While Klein emphasized the chief value of play for its symbolic representation of unconscious material which required to be interpreted before it had value, Winnicott gave to the capacity to play the defining mark of our humanity. 'On the basis of playing', he writes, 'is built the whole of man's experiential existence' (1971: 75).

In leading psychotherapy back into the far older tradition of playing, Winnicott takes up a theme powerfully argued by the cultural historian, Johan Huizinga, in his classic study of play and civilization, *Homo Ludens* (1949). Huizinga's bold thesis is that 'civilization arises and unfolds as play', and he places play as being older even than culture which itself always presupposes human society. He defines play as 'the active principle' beyond 'instinct', through which nothing was explained. He also places it beyond 'mind' or 'will' which, he believed, offered too much by way of explanation. Winnicott, too, claimed that the instincts were the main threat to play as they were to the ego. 'In play', Huizinga claims, 'there is something *at play* which transcends the immediate needs of life and imparts meaning to action'. In a hierarchy of observations that included justice, beauty, truth, goodness, mind and God, Huizinga sees play alone as undeniable in its universality. For him, language was itself the expression of play. 'In giving expression to life, man creates a second poetic world alongside the world of nature.' He points to myth and ritual as bearing the great instinctive forces of civilized life, in which law and order, commerce and profit, craft and art, poetry, wisdom and science all have their origin. 'All', he claims, 'are rooted in the primeval soil of play' (Huizinga 1949: 5).

Huizinga saw play as taking place within an aesthetic order bounded by distinctions in locality and duration, where 'tension, poise, balance, contrast, variation, solution and resolution' were arranged in animated and labile discourse, absorbing the players, as he puts it, 'intensely and utterly'. The vulnerable character of the play-mood is such that its location has to be quite specific.

> The arena, the card-table, the magic circle, the temple, the stage, the screen, the tennis-court, the court of justice, etc. are all in form

and function play-grounds – that is forbidden spots, isolated, hedged round, hallowed, within which special rules obtain . . . All are temporary worlds within the ordinary world dedicated to the performance of an act apart.

(Huizinga 1949: 10)

These distinctive characteristics of play in Huizinga's vision are immediately and arrestingly descriptive of the analytic space, the special setting, 'a place for absent-mindedness', as Marion Milner describes it.

The precariousness of play was a theme shared by Winnicott's; he saw the risks inherent in it, its tension, uncertainty, chanciness. Its opposite is captured in Huizinga's analogous notion, 'ordinary life'. This is where the reality principle, as the psychoanalyst would say, waits all the while to 'reassert its rights either by an impact from without, which interrupts the game, or by an offence against the rules, or else from within, by a collapse of the play spirit, a sobering, a disenchantment' (Huizinga 1949: 21). These are not only distinctive characteristics of the analytic discourse generally; they are voiced by Winnicott in a similar vein when he claims that 'playing is inherently exciting and precarious': a precariousness that belongs to the interplay in the child's mind of that which is subjective (near hallucination) and that which is objectively perceived (actual, or shared reality) (1971: 61).

Marion Milner sees playing in childhood, as well as the freely associative state of undirected activity in adults, as 'an essential recurrent phase of a creative relation to the world', an 'alive stillness'. Huizinga refers to this as the 'disinterestedness' of playing, 'standing outside the immediate satisfaction of wants and appetites'. In fact, he concludes, play 'interrupts the appetitive process . . . interpolating itself as a temporary activity satisfying in itself and ending there'. This prefigures Winnicott's characterization of playing as being essentially satisfying and reaching its own climax, a 'saturation point' which, in Winnicott's words, 'refers to the capacity to contain experience' (1971: 61).

Huizinga recognizes the 'secludedness' of play. He writes, 'Play begins and then at a certain moment it is *over*. It plays itself to an end. While it is in progress all is movement, change, alternation, succession, association, separation' (Huizinga 1949: 9). He captures here the fluidity of another of Winnicott's conceptual paradoxes, 'the separation that is not a separation but a form of union' which governs

Winnicott's concept of the transitional object – the object that is both created by the baby and found, in Winnicott's phrase, 'conveniently lying around' through the mother's highly adaptive presence.

Huizinga makes playing the fundamental mark of civilization; Winnicott echoes this in his later work. Huizinga claims for playing that

> It adorns life, amplifies it and is to that extent a necessity both for the individual – as a life function – and for society by reason of the meaning it contains, its significance, its expressive value, its spiritual and social associations, in short, as a culture function.
>
> (Huizinga 1949: 9)

Huizinga thus sees play as a fundamental form of social life; he concludes his book,

> The spirit of playful competition is, as a social impulse, older than culture itself and pervades all life . . . Ritual grew up in sacred play; music and dancing were pure play. Wisdom and philosophy found expression in words and forms derived from religious contests. The rules of warfare, the conventions of noble living were built up on play-patterns. We have to conclude, therefore, that civilization . . . is played. It does not come *from* play like a babe detaching itself from the womb; it arises *in* and *as* play, and never leaves it.
>
> (Huizinga 1949: 173)

Winnicott, writing in terms of individual development, was making no lesser claim for play than was Huizinga for civilization. In *Playing and Reality*, he writes, 'It is in playing and only in playing that the individual child or adult is able to be creative and to use the whole personality, and it is only in being creative that the individual discovers the self' (1971: 63).

At the very centre of Winnicott's theory of playing lies his concept of potential space – that area in between the inner psychic reality of an individual, bounded by some defining bodily configuration such as 'the mind', 'the guts' or 'the head', and that of external or shared reality, a location outside the personal body scheme. It is only in this area that an individual is free to be creative. It is in this area, too, that he suggested psychotherapy took place. It is in this potential space that he believed communication to be possible at all and it is in the non-purposiveness, the 'disinterestedness' that Huizinga refers to, that the highly sophisticated form of playing that is psychotherapy takes place.

It is quite clear that the non-purposive state for which Winnicott makes such powerful claims can only be achieved in an optimally safe environment, experienced over time by an infant in the mother's highly adaptive and reliable presence. It is a state that might arise through a patient's experiences of the predictable and reliable analytic setting. Just as Winnicott saw unbearable anxiety as destroying playing for the child, so he felt that too great an anxiety on the part of the patient could invade the play area of psychotherapy and interrupt the potential for unconscious communication.

Although Winnicott saw the therapist as a participant in the unfolding of such communications, he also placed the therapist a hair's breadth outside as well. Thus therapists were engaged in play areas of their own, in between their own internal world and that of their patients, whilst, as he put it elsewhere, keeping both their feet on their ground.

For this capacity of civilization – as Huizinga has claimed for play – to find expression both in the matter of childhood play and in that of the psychotherapeutic encounter, the setting, the environmental provision is of the essence. For Winnicott, the maturational processes themselves were dependent on the creativity of the environmental character. For Marion Milner creativity is similarly dependent.

> It requires a physical setting in which we are freed, for the time being, from the need for immediate practical expedient action; it requires a mental setting, an attitude, both in the people around and in oneself, a tolerance of something which may at moments looks very like madness . . . In our childhood we are allowed to act, move, behave, under the influence of illusions, to play 'pretend' games and even get lost in our play, feel for the moment that it is real. In adult life it is less easy to find settings where this is possible (we get other people to do the pretending on the films and the stage), although we do find it within the framework of the analytic setting as patients.

Milner goes on to point out that her clinical experience repeatedly suggested to her that 'many of the impediments to going forward into living are the results of a failure of the child's environment to provide the necessary setting for such absent-mindedness' (Milner 1971: 164), 'absent-mindedness' being her word for Winnicott's 'non-purposive activity' or Huizinga's 'disinterestedness'.

Winnicott locates play as being bounded by distinctions of locality and duration, by the 'secludedness' that Huizinga also distinguishes as being an absolute necessity. 'All play', Huizinga notes in *Homo Ludens*, 'moves and has its being within a playground marked off beforehand either materially or ideally, deliberately or as a matter of course' (Huizinga 1949: 10). Milner emphasizes the extreme vulnerability and fear of the person playing in this way.

All three, Huizinga, Milner and Winnicott, use the word precariousness to communicate the liminal status of this condition. It is worth perhaps noting that the word conveys a state worthy of prayer because of its fluid uncertainty.

In the psychological arena both Winnicott and Milner postulate creativity as having its foundation in this formless functioning. Winnicott, most particularly, lays stress on the vital need for the presence of another highly adaptive individual magically able, from the developing infant's viewpoint, to reflect its own experiencing. For Winnicott, it was only in the highly specialized conditions of friendship or psychoanalysis that playing can take place, that, as he put it, 'the individual can come together and exist as a unit, not as a defence against anxiety but as an expression of I AM, I am alive, I am myself' (1971: 66).

In Winnicott's special sense, then, from this position everything is creative. In these specialized conditions it is as if the child as a unit has implicitly understood for the first time that it has been seen and understood to exist by someone. In Winnicott's words, 'I get back (as a face seen in a mirror) the evidence I need that I have been recognized as a being' (1982b: 61). From this point, the infant can now afford to look into the world, finding there that which has so far existed only in potential as dream material but which it can now find in enriched form in the world of shared experience of all kinds. This permanent dialectical movement from internal to external constitutes the answer that Winnicott gave to his own question as to what life was about, a question at the root of so much philosophic speculation and so little psychoanalytic discourse.

Winnicott made the direct link between childhood playing and the psychotherapeutic task. Therapists, he states, 'afford opportunity for formless experience, and for creative impulses, motor and sensory, which are the stuff of playing. And on the basis of playing is built the whole of man's experiential existence (1971: 75).

THE FAMILIAR IN THE UNFAMILIAR

The essential non-identity between that which is conceived of and that which is waiting to be found in the world – the spatial and temporal elasticity of the potential space of the play area – exerted a special force in the work of both Winnicott and Milner and led Winnicott to conceive of tradition in a particularly dynamic way. Milner, in Winnicott's words, saw this non-identity as 'the primary human predicament' (1951: 391). And more than this. For it was this 'predicament' that led the human being out of a solipsistic encounter with what had already been found, into the arena of creativity where a personal tradition would find its ultimate validity. It is in the sense that individual creativity is essentially original, though embedded in a historic continuity, that enabled Winnicott to regard the individual at play as being both bound by tradition and absolutely original.

In *Playing and Reality*, he brings this paradox vividly to life by asserting,

it is not possible to be original except on a basis of tradition . . . The interplay between originality and the acceptance of tradition as the basis for inventiveness seems to me just one more example, and a very exciting one, of the interplay between separateness and union.
(1971: 117)

This is a statement that almost exactly parallels in its elements his concept of playing and what he has to say about live experiencing.

We experience life in the area of transitional phenomena, in the exciting interweave of subjectivity and objective observation, and in an area that is intermediate between the inner reality of the individual and the shared reality of the world that is external.
(1971: 75)

An examination of any dictionary definition of tradition lays emphasis on the weight of the past in exerting an orientating or even normative influence on the present. Tradition bears the burden of cultural continuity embodied in a massive complex of evolving social attitudes, beliefs, conventions and institutions rooted in the experience of the past. But it is in the interplay, in the potential space between the subjective and that which is objectively perceived, between the past and the present, that we may look to find this striking paradox. In his classic statement on tradition, T. S. Eliot contemplated 'the past as being altered by the present as much as the present by the past' (Eliot 1919: 14).

This complex concomitance of past and present, this diachronic interplay, is what so visibly and recognizably characterizes the transference phenomenon of psychoanalysis. Milner emphasizes the necessity for a handing over of the temporal and logical as a precondition both for her 'free drawing' and for the psychoanalytic encounter itself. This handing over contains the idea of a kind of inner surrendering, a devotional act of giving the self to the creative moment. In psychoanalytic discourse, it is the delicate moment when, in Winnicott's words, the patient is able to hand over his 'false self' into the being of the analyst. It is at this stage that transformation within both analyst and patient can really be said to begin. Once more, this is a precarious moment when both engaged within this space and time are genuinely at risk. The patient is absolutely dependent on the analyst's proccupation with his analysand in the 'secludedness' of the setting, just as the artist is held within the frame of his imagination.

It is at this stage in an analysis that Winnicott notes a particular characteristic of the transference. It bears the quality of timelessness and reintroduces us to the idea of a dynamic temporal dialogism which lies at the heart of his and Eliot's understanding of tradition. Here the analyst must, in Winnicott's words, 'allow the patient's past to be the present'. He goes on,

> whereas in the transference neurosis the past comes into the consulting-room, in this work it is more true to say that the present goes back into the past, or is the past. Thus the analyst finds himself confronted with the patient's primary process in the setting in which it had its original validity.

> (1982a: 298)

This 'original validity' was for Winnicott the point in the nascent individual's life when the self's core had been traumatically invaded, dispossessing it of its own true character by the impingement of the environment's own conscious or unconscious needs. The original validity in which the individual life could once again discover its own character was, for Winnicott, as indeed it was for Freud, the justification for psychoanalytic treatment.

For Winnicott, there was an inevitability that the psychoanalytic transaction should be marked by 'failure' in an analysis that was going well. The failure would be actual, the analyst actually letting his patient down in any of the innumerable ways that become possible in the intricate detail and prolonged time-scale that constitutes an analytic treatment. The interplay of the patient's psyche with the analyst's sufficient commitment to the process, his highly adaptive presence in the unfolding of the patient's past, would bring him to this inevitable reprise. After perhaps years of fruitful, careful reflectedness during the vicissitudes of the patient's development of his own mood and character in this 'secluded' space, the analyst would find himself at a point of unconsciousness within his own play area when he would, indeed, 'fail' his patient. It is about this precious moment – about this point of the interplay of the two play areas, that of the patient and that of the therapist – when the analyst does actually fail his patient, that Winnicott expresses his discovery. It grew out of his ordinary analytic work and undoubtedly enriched theory with its own originality.

When working with certain patients Winnicott found himself using what he called 'primary identification': where the setting itself would be more important than the interpretation. Here, the setting would include the reliability of the analyst's person, details of basic provision and, most particularly, the analyst's continuing non-retaliatory effect, no matter how great the provocation. This amplification of the meaning of the setting was itself a departure from classical theory. He nevertheless continued to follow the basic principle of psychoanalysis where, entirely according to Freud's own elaboration, 'the patient's unconscious leads and is alone to be pursued'. But then Winnicott makes a major contribution to the theoretical field in characteristic fashion. He is talking about failing patients and it is in this same paper that he goes on to make his challenging claim that 'every failed analysis is a failure not of the patient but of the analyst' (1982a: 298), a failure arising presumably from deficits in his own analysis. It is from the acknowledgement of such failures that the analyst may enable the patient, given time, to be angry with him for his failure rather than to be traumatically disrupted. Traumatic discontinuity – the result of an infant having to react to an impingement – would have been the case in the original setting at the beginning. Winnicott describes how the patient uses the analyst's failures in the following way, and in doing so he also demonstrates how he came upon this discovery:

The way that this change comes about from the experience of being disrupted to the experience of anger is a matter that interests me in a special way, as it is at this point in my work that I found myself *surprised*. The patient makes use of the analyst's failures. Failures

there must be, and indeed there is no attempt to give perfect
adaptation . . . Others may be surprised, as I was, to find that
while a gross mistake may do but little harm, a very small error of
judgment may produce a big effect. The clue is that the analyst's
failure is being used and must be treated as a past failure, one that
the patient can perceive and encompass, and be angry about now.

(1982a: 298)

Such discoveries as these, with their own originality, and there were
many, are almost always expressed by Winnicott in terms of surprise – at the spontaneous arrival at an idea which could nevertheless
not have come about had he not been steeped in the psychoanalytic
tradition of Freud.

In a letter to Harry Guntrip where, perhaps unfairly, he takes issue
with what he saw as Ronald Fairbairn's attempt to knock Freud over
in order to put up something in his place, Winnicott clearly states his
own position in regard to originality and tradition:

Any theories that I may have which are original are only valuable
as a growth of ordinary Freudian psychoanalytic theory. My paper
on Regression would make no sense at all if planted on a world that
had not been prepared for it by Freud. In any paper I have written
I simply take for granted that people know their Freud and are
familiar with the developing theory which had to be started off
somewhere.

(1987: 75)

In a letter to Hannah Ries in November 1953, where he is talking
about his work with the less classically neurotic patients encountered
in Freud's day, he reaffirms this seed-bed of his own understanding
and declares, 'there is no point at all in going on to discover new
things if one forgets the old things' (1987: 55).

In a reflective mood when addressing the 1952 Club (the society of
independent senior analysts who met informally for theoretical discussion), Winnicott returned to the theme of his own origins. He told
the meeting,

At the beginning I do know that . . . as soon as I found Freud and
the method he gave us for investigating and for treatment, I was in
line with it . . . I suppose, if there's anything I do that *isn't*
Freudian, this is what I want to know. I don't mind if it isn't, but I
just feel that Freud gave us this method which we can use, and it
doesn't matter what it leads us to. The point is, it *does* lead us to

things; it's an objective way of looking at things and it's for people who can go to something without preconceived notions, which in a sense, is science.

(1989: 574)

This declaration places Winnicott squarely inside the tradition of scientific objectivism while demonstrating his mobile and paradoxical relationship with this older order.

In 1951, Winnicott reviewed Marion Milner's classic work, *On Not Being Able to Paint*, which was first published in 1950 under the pseudonym 'Joanna Field'. This was the period when what became known as the 'Controversial Discussions' between the followers of Klein and those of Anna Freud still formed the critical base of the British psychoanalytic movement. Winnicott used Milner's pioneering ideas on illusion and symbol-formation to underline the manner in which he himself used existing theory to fashion and create his own theories. By analogy, he is once again pointing to the dis-identity between what is perceived and what is conceived of, or, in Milner's words, the dis-identity of 'the inner dream and objective fact'. He tells us in this review that it is Milner who is reminding psychoanalysts and all teachers that teaching is not enough. We may imagine, however, that he regarded the current warring for a dominant cultural ideology in psychoanalysis with alarm and some disdain. He declared,

Each student must create what is there to be taught, and so arrive at each stage of learning in his own way. If he temporarily forgets to acknowledge debts this is easily forgiven, since in place of paying debts he rediscovers with freshness and originality and also with pleasure, and both the student and the subject grow in experience.

(1951: 392)

J.-B. Pontalis makes an especially rewarding contrast between Winnicott and the European tradition of thought and practice. He says,

In France, we are fond of forging 'neo-concepts', if only to separate ourselves off from our masters and colleagues. After all, one applies them, one always finds something to justify their relevance. Winnicott, though, proceeds in the reverse direction: he finds something – difficult cases that have forced him to find it and, as best he can – because he is not a Freudologist – he puts words on to his discovery.

(Clancier and Kalmanovitch 1987: 142)

Pontalis also points to Winnicott's capacity to bring 'to birth the new in given culture'. This capacity, Pontalis believed, derived from the very fact that Winnicott came from outside the European tradition and that he was not 'made to measure for it'. Echoing Winnicott, he further comments, 'A personal tradition helps one to be original, not [to be] *of* the system' (Clancier and Kalmanovitch 1987: 142).

SCIENCE AND NIGHTMARES

For Winnicott, then, as for Jung, a scientific truth was no more than a working hypothesis which might be adequate for the moment but was not to be preserved as an article of truth in perpetuity (Jung 1963). He forcefully expresses in his correspondence and other occasional writings what amounted to an allergy to the party line, to dogma, to banners (1987: 79).

Winnicott saw the scientist, above all, as one 'who knows that no truth is absolute or final, and it is the thinking and the feeling and the freedom to speculate that counts' (1989: 460). He comments that had Melanie Klein been a true scientist she would have disavowed Joan Riviere, foremost follower of Melanie Klein and Winnicott's own analyst, when she stated that Melanie Klein

> has in fact produced something new in psychoanalysis: namely, an *integrated* theory which, though still in outline, nevertheless, takes account of all psychological manifestations, normal and abnormal, from birth to death, and leave no unbridgeable gulfs and no phenomena outstanding without intelligible relation to the rest.
>
> (1989: 460)

Winnicott condemned this approach as not only unscientific and omnipotent but as in some vital way inevitably leading to a foreclosure on all discovery past, present and future. For, in his terms, it was only by the constant re-invention, re-discovery of facts that living experience could be truly embodied by each individual for himself.

Masud Khan saw Winnicott's preoccupation with facts as being peculiarly English. He says,

> For him facts were the reality, theories the human stammer towards grasping facts . . . Nothing [for Winnicott] was given and absolute. Each man had to find and define his own truth. What was given was the experiential spectrum. And it was towards making

sense of his long encounter with the clinical realities that he devoted all his energies.

(Khan 1982: xi)

Winnicott astringently reminds Klein, whom he none the less deeply admired, that no matter what the validity of her contribution may have been, the further understanding that she had been able to bring through her work 'does not bring us towards a narrowing of the field of investigation; as you know, any advance in scientific work achieves an arrival at a new platform from which a wider range of the unknown can be sensed' (1987: 85).

Far more of Winnicott's way of sensing the unknown can be deduced from his partly ironic comment, 'No advance in psychoanalytic theory is made without nightmares. The question is: who is to have the nightmares?' (1989: 458). Perhaps Winnicott's antipathy to Klein's followers lay precisely in what he saw as their attempt to avoid the nightmares inherent in creativity by the imposition of a closed and complete system of thought and theory.

The party line, then, for Winnicott was anathema. And yet, again paradoxically, Winnicott acknowledged that originality could only arise out of a tradition. In this he comes very close to T. S. Eliot's classic statement on tradition:

[Tradition] cannot be inherited . . . and if you want it you must obtain it by great labour. It involves . . . the historical sense . . . and the historical sense involves a perception, not only of the pastness of the past, but of the presence; the historical sense compels a man to write not merely with his own generation in his bones, but with a feeling that the whole of literature of Europe from Homer and within it the whole of the literature of his own country has a simultaneous existence and composes a simultaneous order. Thus historical sense, which is a sense of the timeless as well as of the temporal and of the timeless and temporal together, is what makes a writer traditional. And it is at the same time what makes a writer most acutely conscious of his place in time, of his own contemporaneity.

(Eliot 1919: 14)

THE UNFOLDING OF A THEORY: FROM GUILT TO THE MOMENT OF HOPE

Winnicott has himself made it possible for us to trace how his concept of a personal tradition underpins some of his most important ideas.

It emphasizes the tension in psychoanalytic history between general theory and the uniquely individual contribution. In terms of individual development the capacity to make a unique contribution is itself the outcome of a tension between what is inherent (nature) and what comes to constitute the environment (nurture).

In a paper originally given as part of a series to celebrate the centenary of Freud's birth, he underlines Freud's immense achievement in his marking the paradox 'Only legal guilt refers to a crime; moral guilt refers to inner reality' (1982b: 16). Freud was referring to the fact of guilt residing in unconscious intention. Even here though, Winnicott reminds us that some two hundred years earlier the English political philosopher, Edmund Burke, was writing about guilt residing in the intention and not in the deed itself.

In this paper Winnicott charts the thrust of Freud's formulation of the super-ego with its foundation in his concept of the Oedipus complex, backwards in time. Through Winnicott a fuller understanding becomes possible of the primitive quality of dread that may inhibit the very enactment of instinctual impulses in an infant whose ego has been insufficiently augmented by the mother's adaptive presence.

Winnicott is making explicit here not only his radical notion that babies as young as six months could be ill, but that arrival at the stage of the Oedipus complex was itself an achievement of health. This achievement was made possible by the mother's adaptive presence; by its means the infant could successfully live through his world of subjective objects omnipotently controlled to a world objectively perceived. The compensation for the loss of this subjective omnipotence was the immeasurable enrichment that the world of shared reality had to offer. Winnicott's concept of the destruction of the subjectively conceived object into one objectively conceived formed a radical departure from classical theory, for in this he was claiming that the fantasied destruction of the subjective object itself made for object-constancy and the reality principle. In this way fantasy and reality became engaged in a mutually enriching transaction between inner and outer psychic reality.

We can begin to follow the way Winnicott used Freud's and Klein's theories about guilt to furnish his own singular contribution. In his paper, 'Psychoanalysis and a sense of guilt', he states, 'There is an early history of the super-ego in each individual: the introject may become human and father-like, but in earlier stages the super-ego introjects are subhuman, and indeed are primitive to any degree'

(1982b: 19). He goes on, '[This] lessening of the burden of guilt feelings follows the lessening of repression, or the approach of the patient towards the Oedipus complex'. It is, thus, here that Winnicott is noting that to arrive at the stage of the Oedipus complex – Freud's departure point – 'ambivalence and the toleration of it by the individual implies a considerable degree of growth and health' (1982b: 21).

He then goes on to acknowledge Klein's immense contribution to the understanding of the origins of the capacity for a guilt sense. He saw her contribution as 'an important result of the continued application of Freud's method'. What was original in Klein for Winnicott was that she changed the emphasis in psychoanalysis away from a preoccupation only with health and neurotic ill health to that of an interest in the idea of the individual's value.

It was Freud, though, who, in Winnicott's words, 'paved the way for the understanding of anti-social behaviour and of crime as a *sequel* to unconscious criminal intention and a symptom of the failure in child care' (1958: 28). In this paper and elsewhere, it is possible to see how Winnicott developed both Freud's and Klein's conceptualization of guilt into his own original contribution in this field. He conceived of the antisocial act as belonging to the moment of hope, with the child reaching back over the area of deprivation to the lost object of successful earlier care. It was at the moment of the antisocial act, Winnicott came to believe, that the child sought to rediscover the object's intrinsic capacity to survive maximum destructiveness which would thereby allow the child to reabsorb the categorical difference between fantasied and real destruction.

In the paper titled 'Postscript: DWW on DWW' (1989), which he wrote in 1967, Winnicott reminds us of his inescapable personal proclivity to 'create' what, in fact, was lying around all the time waiting to be found. He could not have created his concept of the antisocial tendency as the moment of hope if Freud and Klein had not been there already, but, in his terms, he did create it whilst elaborating on all that had gone before. 'It's quite possible', he commented, without defensiveness, to the 1952 Club, 'for me to have got this original idea of mine about the anti-social tendency and hope, which has been extremely important to me in my clinical practice, from somewhere. I never know what I've got out of glancing at Ferenczi, for instance, or glancing at a footnote to Freud' (1988: 579). We may detect the note of defiance in this, even, perhaps, Winnicott's own antisocial tendency in seeming to acknowledge theft.

SPONTANEITY, SURPRISE AND DISCOVERY

Winnicott's discovery of powerful and new theoretical insights emerged from his everyday clinical work, with surprise and tentatively, and, as he says, with fright.

> I gave many tentative and frightened papers to colleagues from the mid-twenties onwards pointing out these facts [that babies could be emotionally ill], and eventually my point of view boiled up into a paper (1936) which I called 'Appetite and emotional disorder'. In this I gave samples of the case histories that had to be reconciled somehow with the theory of the Oedipus complex as the point of origin of individual conflicts.
>
> (1982b: 172)

Indeed, reconciliation was not possible as Melanie Klein above all, with her seminal ideas on infantile unconscious phantasy, and Winnicott with his conviction that babies could be emotionally ill, were coming to believe. As they strove to find 'the familiar in the unfamiliar', they moved theory on, enriching all that had gone before, transforming the current analytic culture, living out the 'constant trafficking in illusion' – by which Winnicott understood experience – where there was 'a repeated reaching to the interplay between creativity and that which the world has to offer' (Winnicott 1987: 43).

Deriving from a different cultural and religious tradition, Winnicott looked on the reality principle not as the obstacle but as the ally of the maturational processes in the infant rather than the arena for mastery. He saw in man's vulnerability his true potential for self-enrichment and the enrichment of others, 'from need and desire and not merely for the autonomous gratification of compelling id-impulses through complicity with others' (Khan 1982: xliii).

There is no doubt some significance in the fact that two of the most outstanding figures in the British psychoanalytic movement, contemporaries who found themselves playing in the same arena, Winnicott and Milner, should display striking similarities in the discourse of their discoveries on creativity. Milner vividly portrays the trepidation, precariousness and joy she discovered in her free drawing and Winnicott the fearfulness and surprise with which he found himself declaring so many of his most controversial conceptual ideas.

Winnicott's very considerable theoretical and narrative skills do themselves certainly add to the reader's reception to his ideas. His sense of surprise, of trepidation, of boldness, and apparent spontaneity all convey to the reader the basic optimism that seems to emerge from a well-seated belief in himself. It is as if he were displaying to his readers the gifts of the fortunate infant, which he above all could so beautifully describe, being already confident of a benign reception. This rhetorical skill as well as his mode for making discoveries can be heard in his very phraseology. 'I suddenly realised – in Paris or somewhere – that early isn't deep; that it takes an infant time and development before depth comes in, so that when you're going back to the deepest things you won't get to the beginning' (Winnicott 1989: 581). The paradox once more urges us to struggle with the difficult discovery that Winnicott makes here.

Winnicott describes his alarm at finding himself saying, at a scientific meeting of the British Psycho-analytical Society in the 1940s, 'There is no such thing as a baby' (1982a: 199). He declares his surprise at finding himself staking a claim in the 1960s for the individual's right not to communicate, indeed for the human being to contain a sacred and inviolable core forever incommunicable. It is with surprise that he discovers the use his more borderline patients could make of his failures (1982a: 298). He draws attention to his surprise at finding himself in the middle of a lecture declaring, 'the anti-social act of the delinquent belongs to a moment of hope' (1989: 577). In his 1948 paper, 'Pediatrics and psychiatry', he surprised himself by saying, 'schizophrenia is an environmental deficiency disease' (1982a: 162).

It is entirely in character that Winnicott should claim that the significant and mutative moment in an analysis comes when the child or adult surprises himself. The clever interpretation, arrived at by the analyst in all his potency, does not, in his view, contain the transformational momentum of the individual's discovery of his own truths in his own time within the analytic space and setting.

It is surely also that tension between what the individual can create and that which is lying around waiting to be found, between the subjective object and the object objectively conceived that makes paradox so intrinsically part of Winnicott's system of belief. For him, the creative gesture arose spontaneously both out of the infant's innate zest and eagerness *to find*, and out of his need *to create* the world that was awaiting him. It is not hard, then, to discern that surprise should be the outcome of the creative tension with which Winnicott's paradoxes challenges us.

THEFT AND THE CREATIVE ACT

Very late in his life, Winnicott described to Masud Khan a conversation he had had shortly before with some young Anglican priests who posed with childlike economy an absolutely fundamental question. How, they asked him, could they distinguish those who came to them in distress, whom they could perhaps help by talking, from those whom they should send off to hospital because they were ill? Winnicott's reply was: 'If a person comes and talks to you and, listening to him, you feel he is *boring* you, then he is sick, and needs psychiatric treatment. But if he sustains your interest, no matter how grave his distress or conflict, then you can help him all right' (1982a: 1).

Winnicott, then, used this quickening in his own interest, his spontaneous and eager response to an individual in deep distress, as a diagnostic tool. It indicated for him his and his patient's potential to become engaged in the therapeutic discourse of playing, no matter how gravely disturbed the patient's presentation.

A clinical vignette will serve to convey both the vitality of the therapist–patient interaction and the potency of the reliable setting, for which Winnicott made such fundamental claims. It also seeks to demonstrate what Winnicott meant by the interplay between the two play areas – that of the patient and that of the therapist – which defined his theory of play and of psychotherapy.

For several years, an experienced therapist had regularly brought to her supervisor material of demanding urgency. Her constant refrain to her supervisor was that here was a patient so borderline in his internal structuring, so given to extensive acting out in alarming and bizarre episodes outside the therapy, so extraordinarily uninterested in his therapist's careful and devoted management and interpretation that she was deeply doubtful that she should ever have taken the patient on. None the less, the patient had continued to come for more than five years four times weekly and the therapist and supervisor continued to be interested and to enjoy – some of the time – the vitality in this man's alternative to living which made no more than a passing nod at the external world. The patient sustained both the therapist's and her supervisor's interest although what was often enacted was mad, disturbing and often evidence of a deeply distressed condition in chaotic conflict.

The therapist, encouraged by her supervisor, contained herself by making interpretations, comments, imaginatively entering his world, allowing herself to become caught up in the patient's singular vision whilst all the while keeping a reliable contact with her supervisor through extensive note-taking after her bewildering sessions.

The therapist had always enjoyed her patient's intellectual flamboyance, his mesmeric use of language and his absolute reliability in turning up for his sessions. At some level, she was all the time aware that if only as a witness, a repository, she was affording this man a first-ever experience of steadiness in the face of catastrophic internal dislocation. Both the patient's parents had been psychiatrically ill, in Winnicott's sense, and had spent long periods in hospital during a large part of the patient's childhood.

Eventually, the therapist noticed in one session that she was falling into a kind of trance as she listened to her patient's extensive philosophic murmurings on the human condition. She found herself gradually becoming caught up in his description of a theoretical framework whose aesthetic and intellectual configuration had had a profound influence on her own work when she had first begun to understand the intimate association of playing and psychotherapy elucidated by Winnicott. The therapist had absolutely no doubt that her patient had never read Winnicott's work. Nevertheless, he was able to convey to her the richness and sophistication of *Playing and Reality*, that most dense and mature theoretical work of Winnicott's last years, in a way that had the therapist wishing that she had been able to make notes. She was astonished at hearing the patient describe his struggle to contain the tensions of infant play as described in Winnicott's controversial and paradoxical conceptualization of this earliest of cultural experiences.

An extract from the session seeks to give the flavour of the patient's speculations: 'What would the world be like if it was a matter of finding in the world only the artefacts of your own experience . . . How would anything get deeper . . . How would anything change . . . What would prevent the gradual degradation of imagination into entropy . . . I don't really notice anything that's there if I haven't imagined it . . . I'm just not interested . . . I don't care . . .' Pause. 'It would be very different if there were consequences to my actions. I'd have to acknowledge something then . . . I'd have to be connected up to the world in a quite different way. I'd have to take care to see what was there . . . I'd have to notice.' Pause. 'That makes me feel afraid. I don't know why.' Pause. 'I don't know whether I mean what I've just said or if you've said something like it to me before and I'm just saying what I've heard you say . . . I don't remember . . . It doesn't feel like it.'

The therapist, disconcerted at the appositeness of the patient's remarks, reported that she was only just able to comment on how he had just then somehow been able to put together a great deal of what they were, one way or another, always talking about; how he and the world might enrich and be enriched by each other.

The young man had been referred to her because the physician treating him for an organic illness was puzzled at his incapacity to follow his treatment plan, despite his high intelligence. Indeed, unbeknown to the doctor, he was busy elaborating his illness by a complicated and obscure pharmaceutical plan of his own, which brought about a satisfying number of inexplicable crises – inexplicable, at least, to the doctor. What was of very considerable concern to the therapist – and, at the time, only to her and her supervisor – was the danger that the patient would succeed in irreversible damage before she and he had established an acceptable treatment plan of their own. From the patient's point of view, he was embarked on a game, unmarked by concern, just as a child might become preoccupied in carefully removing the wings from a wasp in an experimental day-dream.

The theoretical distinction that Winnicott makes between fantasizing and dreaming and real living is markedly relevant here. This patient's capacity for fantasizing had reduced him into being, in Winnicott's words, 'creative into space', isolated in a kind of autism, his energies being absorbed by this activity, but of no value to him for living or for dreaming. Indeed, so lost did he become in his distraction from the reality principle that he did almost manage to kill himself. At this time, it had occurred to him to stop all his medication, as drugs no longer seemed to him to be of any consequence. He had become bored with this game. Fortunately, absolute unconsciousness supervened and carried him to hospital, and to the provision of basic care that he needed in the absence of his therapist, who was on holiday at the time.

His marked lack of concern for outcome (and here I am using Winnicott's development of Melanie Klein's concept of the depressive position) is what marks off his activities from that of playing. There was no interplay – however minute – of external reality being brought to bear on a piece of his internal world. His activities were only imitative of that conjunction, in effect reflecting an indiscriminate borrowing from an external world not yet acknowledged as such and hence not part of a healthy conjunction between external reality and inner psychic reality.

In a statement of the earliest possible interplay between internal and external worlds, Winnicott made the following statement of the infant embarked on creating the world:

> Into this play area the child gathers objects or phenomena from external reality and uses these in the service of some sample derived from inner or personal reality. Without hallucinating the child puts out a sample of dream potential and lives with this sample in a chosen setting of fragments from external reality.
>
> (1971: 60)

This patient, after many dangerous and difficult years, has begun to acknowledge some of his dependency on his therapist's presence. For many years, she had reported a kind of parallel presence between herself and her patient, with very little tendency of the two play areas coinciding. However, the patient's extraordinary encapsulation of Winnicott's most complex ideas, unconsciously derived from the unspoken texts of his therapist's own conceptual framework, unexpectedly provoked the patient to question himself aloud as to whether he had himself originated this theory or whether he had stolen it from his therapist. In a most particular way, of course, he had done both! He had, unconsciously, also gathered on his way, in this act, what Winnicott had to say about the hopefulness contained in the antisocial gesture, with the capacity to steal, in his case, a developmental achievement of consequence.

Here, perhaps, we can understand the perspicuity of Masud Khan's claim for Winnicott – as well as for himself – when he says, 'the analyst and the patient are part of a larger total process . . . in which each is being ''created'' and ''found'' by the other'. It is this mutuality and reciprocity, 'the dialogic dynamism which is more than object-relating in the transference' (Khan 1975: xxi), that is arrestingly illustrated in the above clinical vignette.

WINNICOTT'S PERSONAL TRADITION

It was Winnicott's contention that psychotherapy could only take place if the patient and the therapist were able to play, to participate each in the other's world, and so create a new shared world in which both would be enriched by the inter-penetration of their experiencing. Winnicott believed this capacity to play to be inherent in human

development, but liable to be arrested if the environment, the
mother, in this case, too importunately impinged on her infant's
maturational processes. It is in this sense that Winnicott so
vehemently resisted the idea, enshrined by some of Klein's followers,
that the therapist alone held the key to the patient's unfolding. For
Winnicott it is the patient and only the patient who bears the spring of
his own destiny; the therapist's task is to provide the sophisticated
and highly specialized milieu. In a lighter moment in the crucial
engagement between these two traditions Winnicott castigated a
colleague for his shortsightedness. 'One felt that if he were growing a
daffodil he would think that he was making the daffodil out of a bulb
instead of enabling the bulb to develop into a daffodil by good enough
nurture' (1987: 35).

The psychiatrist J. H. Khan, writing in the *British Journal of
Psychiatry* a year after Winnicott's death, captures the sense in which
Winnicott's contribution to psychoanalytic thought and practice was
truly original and shows how, at the same time, he was a messenger
from the far older tradition of playing. He describes how Winnicott
witnessed and encouraged the birth of something new, distinctive and
unanticipated, from the oldest form of symbolic thought transmission, the drawing of representational lines. J. H. Khan writes,

> The message which Winnicott transmitted to his students were
> themselves like his squiggles. A single line, or dot, or word, added
> by his patient or student collaborator, gave it a meaning which
> could never be anticipated. It was a creation of the moment, and in
> this interacting way each listener or reader achieved a benefit
> which Winnicott did not claim to have offered.
>
> (Khan 1972: 119)

Perhaps the final word may, though, be given to Masud Khan, editor
of Winnicott's published works during his lifetime, who best conveys
the paradox that lies within Winnicott's concept of the personal tradition: 'Each of us who has encountered him has his *own* Winnicott, and
he never transgressed the other's invention of him by any assertion of
his own style of being. And yet he always stayed so inexorably
Winnicott' (Khan 1982: xi).

Clare Winnicott remembered her husband as always reading
Freud and that he was 'never without a book of Freud's' (Rudnytsky
1991: 190). Winnicott's work certainly could not have emerged
without his Freudian inheritance. Nevertheless, it is his personal
experience of seeing 60,000 mothers and children over forty years

as a pediatrician that has undoubtedly made his personal tradition utterly unique.

REFERENCES

Bollas, C. (1987) *The Shadow of the Object: Psychoanalysis of the Unthought Known*, London: Free Association Books.

Clancier, A. and Kalmanovitch, J. (1987) *Winnicott and Paradox: from Birth to Creation*, London: Tavistock Publications.

Eliot, T. S. (1953) 'Tradition and the individual talent', in *Selected Essays*, London: Faber & Faber.

Huizinga, J. (1949) *Homo Ludens: a Study of the Play Element in Culture*, London: Routledge & Kegan Paul.

Jung, C. G. (1963) *Memories, Dreams and Reflections*, London: Collins, Routledge & Kegan Paul.

Khan, J. H. (1972) 'Tribute to Donald Winnicott', *British Journal of Psychiatry* 120: 119–20.

Khan, Masud (1982) 'Introduction', in D. W. Winnicott's *Through Paediatrics to Psychoanalysis*, London: Hogarth Press and the Institute of Psychoanalysis.

Milner, M. (1971) *On Not Being Able to Paint*, London: Heinemann.

—— (1987) *The Suppressed Madness of Sane Men*, London: Tavistock Publications.

Rudnytsky, P. (1991) *The Psychoanalytic Vocation: Rank, Winnicott and the Legacy of Freud*, London: Yale University Press.

Winnicott, D. W. (1951) Critical notice of *On Not Being Able to Paint*, in *Psychoanalytic Explorations* (1989), London: Karnac Books.

—— (1971) *Playing and Reality*, London: Tavistock Publications.

—— (1982a) *Through Paediatrics to Psychoanalysis*, London: Hogarth Press and the Institute of Psychoanalysis.

—— (1982b) *The Maturational Processes and the Facilitating Environment*, London: Hogarth Press and the Institute of Psychoanalysis.

—— (1987) *The Spontaneous Gesture: Selected Letters of D. W. Winnicott*, ed. by R. Rodman, London: Harvard University Press.

—— (1989) *Psychoanalytic Explorations*, ed. by D. W. Winnicott, C. Shepherd, and R. and M. Davis, London: Karnac Books.

Chapter 5

The sceptical tradition in psychotherapy

J. M. Heaton

Psychotherapy has a long tradition and its origins, like those of any deep tradition, are lost in the mists of time. For human beings have a natural desire to tend and help those who are in pain and distress and this desire is the source from which flows the practice of medicine and psychotherapy. As time has gone by things have become much more complicated. Thus it has been found that some people are more skilled at using the resources of the material world to help and others at using the cultural world, language and symbols. And experience has taught us that some conditions respond better if treated by material means, others by cultural means, and others by either one or by both, the psychosomatic disorders being an example. And most important of all we have come to realize that helping people is a lucrative way of earning a living. Nevertheless, at the heart of the practice of therapy is the desire to be of help.

Psychotherapy, the cure of souls, helping people who are anxious and confused about the meaning of what is happening to them, is an ancient and sophisticated occupation, as is shown by a reading of the ancient Egyptian pyramid texts carved on the walls of the pyramid of King Wenis around 2300 BC. Traditional thinking has a deep respect for this venerable experience. One thing it teaches is the huge variety of ways of helping people and how the kind of help and its assessment depends on the notion of the soul, mind and spirit that the sufferer and his helper live by.

But this respect for the past and its differences has been broken. In the western tradition in medicine a profound split has occurred, owing to the influence of the Enlightenment. This split was the result of the rejection of traditional thinking and its replacement with fields of knowledge. The sciences are our prime example of fields of knowledge. Kant defined a science as a system in its own right that 'architecturally' must be treated as a 'self-subsisting whole . . . a separate and independent building . . . and not as a wing or section of another [one]' (Kant 1790: Ch. 68). So the roots of medicine are now seen to lie in the sciences: physiology, biochemistry, psychology, sociology, etc. One kind of knowledge, medicine, is given priority in assessing human nature and meaning. Other approaches as to what is cure, what is health, what is the most effective expression of the desire to help, are pushed to the background. Questions about human nature are replaced by the idea of normality, that is what is usual or typical is assumed to be how things ought to be (Hacking 1990). Medicine becomes an applied science.

The great significance of Freud and Jung is that they claimed to found a science of psychotherapy, that is, a separate discipline. It was based on a theory and a technique that made possible the development of knowledge and so could transform its object of knowledge in a specific practice. So the practice becomes subordinate to the theory and the knowledge which is accumulated. This has the enormous advantage that it opened the way for technicians to be trained in the theory, knowledge and practice. However the really serious task of each individual, that of thinking for himself, which does not mean by himself, and so clarifying his own and others' nature and desire to help, can be passed by. For the theory tells them the norm.

Time and again Freud calls himself a theoretician, claiming that cure and the analytic method are only authentic because they are based on a scientific theory. The cures of non-psychoanalytic psychotherapists, as opposed to psychoanalysts, are not genuine but only suggestive, since they have no theory. Even if all neurosis and psychosis is eventually cured by drugs, as Freud believed would happen, psychoanalysis would still be fully justified because of the knowledge of the human mind it gave us. Variations on this belief are repeated by the founders of the different schools of psychoanalysis.

Now there is a long tradition in philosophy and medicine which argues that practice is more fundamental than theory or knowledge. This tradition in philosophy is known as Pyrrhonian scepticism and in medicine as the Methodical School, one of the three main schools of ancient medicine. Both branches of this tradition were centrally concerned with the nature of therapy, the origin and scope of knowledge and its relation to therapy, the critique of dogmas and theories, and the way to respond to conflicts between beliefs to attain tranquillity. Above all they were concerned to base their activities on practice rather than on a body of doctrines. I will try to show that their example and arguments are highly relevant to psychotherapy today and that the pseudo-sciences of psychoanalysis, analytic psychology, psychosynthesis, Gestalt psychology, etc., all of which are founded on theory and dogma, stand in the way of getting a clear understanding of the practice of psychotherapy and its relation to tradition.

TRADITION

It is first necessary to clarify what is meant by traditional thinking, as most modern criticisms of tradition depend on confusions about it. The word 'tradition' comes from the Latin *tradere* to hand over, pass on, or, if reflexive, to put oneself at the disposal of. The traditional thinker does not found something himself and then worry about how to pass it on but is concerned with that which is essentially passed on or received. He is at the disposal of that which he himself and his culture is essentially part of. So the origin of a deep tradition is such that no one can have been present at its birth; it has to be expressed in mythical terms. Thus at the source of Greek medicine we have mythical figures such as Apollo, Chiron, Asclepius.

Tradition must be differentiated from custom. 'Custom' comes from the Latin *consuescere*, meaning to become accustomed or used to a state of affairs, to be in the habit of. So customs are not necessarily traditional, for an individual may start a custom or force people to become accustomed to a state of affairs. Good habits can be taught, a tradition is uncovered.

A tradition is not something we can learn, we cannot pick one up when we feel like it or choose one and reject another any more than we can choose our own ancestors. But we can learn customs and choose to inculcate habits. Tradition is part of being human, we all stand within one and it is that which is most familiar, for it hands down our own possibilities. But humans also create customs and these can be individually confronted in a free and detached way, in contrast to tradition. Conflicts about the justification of a particular custom cannot be resolved merely by appealing to custom; justification has its source in tradition. Thus it was a custom in China to bind women's feet; this was eventually criticized and abolished. But this has not led to the abolishing of Chinese traditions. A tradition is not an object we can confront for we are always subject to its effects. It does not develop but shifts and changes.

Tradition becomes stultifying when it hardens into a deposit of sedimented knowledge which appears self-evident, when we forget the vital element which makes it a living tradition. To retrieve, or bring to the surface, this sediment is not simply to reiterate something past or to imitate it but is to reveal the hitherto hidden possibilities of meaning that it offers. This retrieving keeps the tradition alive.

The retrieval is not continuing the past by the methods of the past but is a return to it, to think it more originally with all the insecurity that a true beginning entails. It is to draw out new possibilities from old origins. This thinking cannot be construed as a method that is laid down prior to the thinking but is rather a 'way', an assignment, as it is empowered by the possibilities that the thinker finds in his inherited situation. It seeks to reveal the possibilities of the past which are in having been, as man is a being who is as having been. Human beings do not live in the pure present but are given the past as the future approaches.

In traditional thinking we may study the past to see what it has to say to us now. We do not shake off tradition, but overcome present ways of thinking by reviving the hidden resources that tradition retains from older ways of thought. This respect for the past is very different from approaches to the past that have become common since the Enlightenment and which Freud and Jung took over and developed.

The endeavour of the thinkers of the Enlightenment was to overcome traditional thinking, especially religious, and build on clear, rational ideas. They thus hoped to found a new era of intellectual freedom and adventure free of all superstition. Marx and Freud are two of the greatest representatives of this way of thought. Freud was happy to think of himself as having the temperament of a *conquistador*, an adventurer who ruthlessly conquered the Incas, a supposedly superstitious and traditional society.

Enlightenment thinkers were concerned to secure scientific knowledge as the most certain form of knowledge, replacing traditional notions like faith and trust. Descartes was the pioneer in this endeavour. To put it briefly, the mind was assumed to be a self-contained sphere of enquiry. A para-mechanical account of mental processes was given which would underwrite some claims to knowledge, for example, the claims of religious knowledge, and disallow others. A causal account of mental processes was added which can justify knowledge claims. To get this programme going it was necessary to replace the older notion of personhood and replace it with the 'space' of consciousness, which developed into the inner world of psychoanalysis. Older notions of persons who necessarily possess moral dignity were replaced by the value of science and the genius of those who create a science. Freud, for example, considered ethics subordinate to psychoanalysis and he, like Marx, considered that he was founding a new science.

A basic assumption of thinkers of the Enlightenment was that certain forms of mental activity were primitive forms, destined to perish when mind reached maturity. According to Vico, who was working in Naples in the early eighteenth century, poetry was the natural mode in which the savage or childish mind expressed itself. As man developed, a mythical or semi-imaginative mode replaced the poetic and was expressed in religion. Finally poetry would be completely replaced by prose and the result would be the adult prosaic and purely rational mode. This theory was taken over and elaborated by Marx and Freud, who used the theory of evolution to strengthen their case.

When we have this picture in mind the past takes on a particular 'look'. It seems to stretch behind us in a continuous line and we become interested in representing the events in their chronological order of occurrence like beads on a string. Freud, for example, tried to fill in the gaps in his patient's memory of past events in order to make a continuous story based on causality. This required judicious handling of evidence and careful attention to explanations as to why and how the particular events in the sequence occurred. It is basically a story in which we are the culmination.

This view of time and history is simply one way of understanding them. For example, the Maori of New Zealand override the distinction between the past and the present and conceive of the future as 'behind' them. We think it obvious that once an event has occurred, it never returns. But to them this is exactly what does happen; the very experiences of the past are the way the present is experienced: 'It was a source of pure, unadulterated joy for the old time Maori, to be able to say to an enemy, "I ate your father" or "your ancestor", although the occurrence may have occurred ten generations before his time' (Best, quoted in Sahlins 1987: 59). The point is that there is no way of standing outside our time and judging that one way of experiencing time is inherently superior to another.

Freud, however, was convinced that modern scientific European man, especially if he had been psychoanalysed, was the culmination of evolution so far. The past, according to this view, is always inferior. Progress is the key word and progress is towards rationality and rationality is thought of in terms of scientific reason, or rather

Freud's understanding of it. So the past is always explained in terms of the superior contemporary present. Freud's system is riddled with these ideas and key notions are interpreted in terms of progress and development. So normal people are superior to neurotics; neurotics to psychotics; men to women; adults to children; modern Europeans to savages; heterosexuals to homosexuals; and, of course, those who have been analysed to those who have not.

Freud, with the boldness of a child of the Enlightenment, declared that psychoanalysis delivered the most wounding blow of all to man's naïve self-confidence in that it proved to the ego that it was not even master in its own house (Freud 1973: 326). He goes on to complain that this blow to our megalomania is the reason that psychoanalysis is so unappreciated! But he does not ask himself who is declaring this, with such grandiose confidence in his own reason. A constant theme of ancient and savage thought is that we are all the playthings of strange forces which need to be assuaged by prayer and sacrifice; more than two thousand years ago sceptics were revealing the frailty of reason. It is characteristic of Freud's rationality that it is so unself-conscious and can boldly step forth and advance and never look over its shoulder.

Evolution, a key concept used by Freud to persuade people that his idea of progress was based on science, was a theory that Darwin applied to nature, not to culture. Huge cultural changes can occur in the course of a few thousand years but this stretch of time is minute when considering the time scale of evolution in nature. If a new-born neolithic infant were somehow transposed with a present-day new-born the subsequent physical, psychological and social development of both would probably be commensurate with their new-found peers. The biological evolution of the brain cannot be directly compared with 'progress' in cultural practices. If a culture put great value on playing chess then most members would become skilled players, but this would not mean they had evolved more than members of a culture that did not play.

Evolutionary biology does not hold any guarantee that there is any main road of progress, still less that we are on it. The proposition, 'Every living thing is caught up in some progressive change' must be carefully distinguished from the proposition, 'There is a single all-embracing process of progressive change in which all living things are caught up.' Science cannot discover 'progress' in itself. I argue that the concept of tradition, which is only applicable to cultures, is far more helpful in understanding psychotherapy, than the concepts of evolution and progress on which psychoanalysis depends.

If right reason is held to belong to one man and his followers, as in the case of psychoanalysis, then problems arise as to how this delicate plant is to be transmitted. It can only be done by using some form of violence. Jealousy, demand for privileged recognition, competitiveness were all encouraged by Freud in a mock innocent way. He even rationalized it by describing his disciples as a savage horde and discussing, in *Totem and Taboo*, how it was necessary for the sons to kill each other in order to take the place of the father!

Perhaps a more sinister method is to analyse one's own children, as Freud did with his daughter Anna; it was successful, in that she remained a dutiful daughter. Klein analysed her three children but was not so successful in that the one who became an analyst later in life turned violently against both her mother and psychoanalysis. Freud and Klein thought that all children should be analysed for prophylactic reasons. They produced no evidence that analysis in childhood prevents neurosis; it just must do so, they thought; their theory predicted it. As Enlightenment thinkers they assumed psychoanalysis was superior even to their own parental love. However, compulsory psychoanalysis would be a good way to propagate the discipline and at the same time destroy the fresh responses of a new generation. In the meantime psychoanalysts have to content themselves with a bureaucracy – the International Psychoanalytical Association – whose business is to instruct and admonish, spot heresy and foster submission to the cause, as it did when banning, without debate, Lacan's teaching.

Tradition has no such problems as it is not the possession of any person or group; it cannot become a cause. Customs and habits can be taught and enforced but tradition cannot, as it is not definable, and there is always the question about what is the genuine and most vital way for it to move and develop. For the time of tradition is not a continuity, it is not concerned with reviving the past.

The classical is the most resistant part of a tradition, since it has a validity that is preserved and handed down. It is defined by Hegel (1975: 427) as 'that which signifies itself and hence also interprets itself'. So it speaks in such a way that it is not a statement about what is past; it speaks to the present as if addressing it specially. Its timelessness therefore is a mode of historical being, so what it says cannot be grasped as a timeless truth possessed by some man or bureaucracy; the actual text however can be forced on people.

Psychoanalysis, by ignoring the conditions that make it possible, and claiming to have the pure gold of therapy in its grasp, is impotent before the power of the prejudices that unconsciously dominate it, as a *vis a tergo*. It has a naïve faith that it can stand above tradition and so make it an object, that is, confront it in a free and detached way by methodically excluding all desire and suggestion and so discover what it contains. But it thereby detaches itself from the continuing action of tradition on which itself depends. And this tradition continues to act through language, to which we must now turn.

LANGUAGE AND TRADITION

Psychotherapy is a remedial discourse. In many ways it can be likened to a ritual in that it is a ceremony that re-enacts the traumas and the loving and hostile wishes of infancy and childhood in a constant setting or space. This re-enactment must be efficacious and so there must be potency in the present act which recalls the past for the purpose of re-ordering the future.

This power does not lie in the strength of the analyst's ego but in the transformational powers of language that are evoked by the meeting of therapist and patient. The charm of language releases the patient from his bewitchment by language. It is through the power of tradition that language acts.

Psychotherapy should concern itself with the practical action of language. It contrasts with psychoanalysis in its various forms, which base themselves on theories of the mind. The psychoanalytic view of language is admirably summarized in an editorial: 'We represent our reality by means of theory and models . . . Language plays a very important role in processing and in transmitting thoughts. But it is dependent upon the particular theoretical model we use and this may mean that we will restrict our exploration of reality' (Editorial 1984: 1). The only use of language recognized here is to represent what has been explored.

But language has many other uses, one of the most important being that words can be acts. Thus to say, 'I am wiggling my toes' is merely a report, but to say, 'I promise' is to promise. In saying, 'I promise', we are not merely representing promising but doing it. The same is true for many phrases in the first person present indicative, perhaps the commonest grammatical form used by the patient in psychotherapy. Thus 'I order', 'I assume', 'I give', 'I affirm', 'I deny', 'I choose', 'I recognize' are all acts. That most important act of declaring love is a speech act in which we put ourselves at risk; it is not merely a report of a feeling or state or thought in the mind, which is put into words and transmitted to the one we love. Understanding love in terms of mental mechanisms such as projective identification completely falsifies the use of language in love, for it assumes language simply clothes our thoughts accurately or falsely.

Psychotherapy depends on the cultural and traditional world in which the patient and therapist live and have their being. Conversation, the way we move people and are moved, the power of language, all depend on the cultural regularities and values embodied in our use of language.

The theorist apprehends action as a spectacle, a representation, a reality to be held at a distance and which is held before him as an object, because he has at his disposal instruments of objectification such as the grid of his theory. In psychoanalysis it leads to lack of clarity about the relation between the theory and what is theorized. For theory is to be written down and this transforms by transcription and interpretation. When a therapy session is described and theorized one passes from a mimetic practice to a philological relation. The session becomes a pretext for decipherment, the need for theoretical coherence and symmetry appears, linked to professional communication, discussion and comparison. This distortion is then played back into further sessions as theory guides practice.

Practice on the other hand acts in urgency; what is at stake is different from theory, its concern is with efficacy rather than rationality. In practice the 'feel for the game' is all important; the way things unfold in time, rhythm, tempo and directionality is constitutive of meaning. Practice is inseparable from a subtle temporality because it is played out in time, and also it plays with time and especially with tempo. And this timing cannot be generalized, since it is game-specific. One may have a marvellous sense of timing in tennis but not in politics or even golf. Theory has a time but it is not that of practice. The theoretician knows what has happened, he sees all, so he can totalize. The player who is involved adjusts not to what he sees but to what he foresees; he anticipates. He decides in response to the overall, instantaneous assessment of the situation: 'on the spot', 'in the twinkling of an eye', 'in the heat of the moment'. These are terms which are more expressive and accurate than hosts of theoretical ones. It is the ability to make these finely honed responses with genuineness that is at the heart of psychotherapy.

An illustration of the problems of theory and practice are psychological theories of war and conflict. Nearly every psychological school has its theory of war. But of what use are they other than to act as an advertisement for the particular school? A peaceful person who might mediate between warring parties must be trusted and respected by both. But trust is essentially a practical matter; it depends on our knowledge of mankind and imponderable evidence such as subtleties of glance, of gesture, of tone. A person may have a wonderful theory but one may not judge that he is a peaceful person. He may be strongly biased towards his theory and so fight for it. But trust is not enough, one may trust an idiot but not to mediate on a matter of great concern. The parties must also feel that the mediator understands what is at stake for them. It is difficult to see how a theory of war aids this, for the mediator is likely to be more interested in the stakes of his theory.

Theory does not teach us to 'wait on' the phenomena at issue in therapy. It is fatal in therapy to satisfy a want which is not yet felt, so that, without waiting till the want is present, one anticipates it. But theory acts like a stimulant to bring about something which is supposed to be a want and then satisfies it. Theory becomes like an addictive drug which cheats people out of what constitutes the significance of life.

Freud complained that philosophers and writers made up their own psychology for themselves: 'everyone has a mental life so everyone regards himself as a psychologist', 'it runs wild', 'there is no technical knowledge' amongst such people (Freud 1926: 179–258). He wanted to turn this polyphony of voices into a monologue. As he wrote to Ferenczi, on 13 May 1913, 'We possess the truth' (Freud 1961).

Freud's monologue has led to a splitting into dozens of branches of psychoanalysis, each with its own theory, particular jargon, and eager followers anxious to propagate 'the truth'. The irony is that neither philosophy nor literature is a confusion of tongues, for most writers in these disciplines do not claim to possess the truth and their truth does not depend on the number of their followers. They are embedded in a tradition and tradition flourishes in different voices from which human truth can flash forth.

Monologue seeks to have the last word, it demands recognition not response. To it another person remains merely an object of consciousness; it is deaf to the other's response and does not acknowledge in it any decisive force. Freud, as his biographers make clear, was not interested in discussing his 'findings' even with his colleagues but he badly wanted recognition.

If a layman tells an inorganic chemist that water is composed partly of nitrogen then an argument or dialogue is not likely to be fruitful; rather, the layman is best told to go off and learn some chemistry. But does the same apply to one's own mind? Surely we all suffer, at times feel lonely, anxious, envious and greedy. We all know our self-pity, vanities, arrogance, search for position and power. These are not possessions of any one person or group nor are they processes going on in the private theatre of our minds which only experts can know. They are shared by all human beings and are part of our common heritage. It is this sharing that makes psychotherapy possible.

Most people have found that self-examination is a difficult and humbling experience; if we are lucky we will do no worse than realize that we don't come up to much. Great traditional thinkers such as Augustine, Montaigne, Pascal, Wittgenstein, all found how little they knew and how shaky were the foundations of knowledge. Freud's self-analysis, the linchpin of his whole system, had quite the opposite effect. He found a method to grasp power.

What he did was to generalize from his own experience, assuming that everyone was like him and that the way to self-knowledge was to follow him or his disciples. He wrote, 'I can only analyse myself with objectively acquired knowledge (as if I were a stranger)' (Masson 1985: 281). He seems to have lacked the ability for intimacy with himself or with others. He was the 'master' even of himself, as his own analysis was always under the control of his ego. As Anzieu remarks, 'His main aim was knowledge not so much of the self as of general, normal psychical processes' (Anzieu 1986: 568). Again, as Anzieu points out, the aim of training analysis is not to enable the student to become intimate with himself but to 'incite in the subject an introjective identification with the psychoanalyst in the form of an ego capable of self-analysis' (ibid.: 570). Freud had no notion of difference, the problem of the Other. He assumed there are universal inner states common to all mankind, a completely unproven and dubious hypothesis (Needham 1981: 53).

The view we have of ourselves is a work of our imagination, as Freud himself realized at times. But he tended to confuse the notion of objective knowledge, which is based on the rules of scientific method and evidence, with the 'composure of mind which no selfishness can disturb' (Wordworth 1964: 744), which is necessary to judge critically works of the imagination. 'For to be mistaught is worse than to be untaught; and no perverseness equals that which is supported by system, no errors are so difficult to root out as those which the understanding has pledged its credit to uphold' (ibid.).

Tradition teaches that there is no last word about the nature of man. Man is on the threshold and it is at the point of contact between people that a light may flash. But monologue transforms this division and play into one continuous text, it erases the speaking voices and puts theory in their place. Freud sought to obliterate authors as bearers of others' words and replace contextual meaning with an absolute psychoanalytical theory.

Tradition is carried by language, it is our mother tongue. The sound of our language; the physiognomy of words; their etymology; the speech gesture; body language – the expression in the eyes, face, hands, the way the body is carried; the nuances and twists of style; intonation – all these carry a tradition which is the matrix within which we understand one another and ourselves. There is an enormous variety of ways in which we use language: requests, demands, orders, confessions of love, chat, squabbling and abuse, exchange of courtesies, intimate communications, professional communications, military commands, legal contracts. They are boundless because the various possibilities of human activity are inexhaustible. We all express ourselves in our way of speaking and using language, drawing on its tradition in various ways to express our persons, our pities, vanities, hates and loves. A one-sided orientation towards one use, say the scientific use, or its use in representing and describing, inevitably leads to a monological distortion of the whole; it just does not sound right.

Tradition is also carried by practices in which discourse is usually essential. Customs, telling fairy stories and tales, gnomic sayings and proverbs, novels, films, computer games, exchange of gifts, orders of respect, modes of kinship, division of labour, the celebration of transitions like birth, adolescence, marriage, death; laws about thresholds such as the entrance to one's house and what can and what cannot enter the various bodily orifices – these all have their particular logic based on tradition. Cultures vary enormously in how they understand these, their rhythms, and the weight of meaning they hold. Psychotherapy must be manifold, subtle, incisive and lucid, in order to understand and play these differences.

THE SCEPTICAL TRADITION

We will now turn to the Pyrrhonian sceptics to indicate their relevance to psychotherapy and tradition. When Freud criticizes philosophy he claims that it behaves like science and works in part by the same methods, but it is defective, 'clinging to the illusion of being able to present a picture of the universe which is without gaps and is coherent, though one that is bound to collapse with every fresh advance in our knowledge' (Freud 1966: 158). He himself whole-heartedly embraced what he calls the '*Weltanschauung* of science' (Freud 1966: 158–82). Freud's magisterial dismissal of philosophy is interesting, for he turned a blind eye to scepticism, assuming that philosophy only builds pictures of the universe. Yet scepticism is hardly of minor significance to philosophy; one could say that most philosophers have thought about it, the majority trying to refute it, the rest being sceptics in one form or another. Sceptics have questioned all the beliefs that Freud mentions: that knowledge and science lead to truth in all areas of human interest, that pictures of the universe are true, that coherence is a universal and necessarily leads to truth. A sketch of the history of scepticism will help show its relevance to psychotherapy.

The word sceptic derives from the Greek *skeptikos* meaning 'thought-ful', 'reflective', 'paying attention to'. Pyrrhonian scepticism is named after a Greek, Pyrrho, who died in 270 BC. He left no written works but was honoured greatly for the purity of his life, so much so that his native city voted that all philosophers should be exempt from taxation! Pyrrho accompanied Alexander to India and is said to have learned from the Indian sages and the Magi. Pyrrhonian scepticism has many similarities to important schools of Indian and Chinese thought, which will not be pursued here. Pyrrhonists never claimed that Pyrrho founded a school; they traced his way of thinking to Plato's dialogues, especially the early ones, to Homer, and the some-what mythical seven wise men. Scepticism is a deep tradition, and its way of thought has been natural to some people in many cultures at least as far back as 1000 BC; it has not had to depend on any bureaucracy to hand it down.

Scepticism in the early days was severely practical. It was a way of life that led to tranquillity of spirit, and in such tranquillity human well-being is found. For example, Anaxarchus, a contemporary of Pyrrho, succeeded in diverting Alexander from thinking he was a god; he treated omnipotent fantasies. Because he criticized the tyrant king of Cyprus he was seized by him and ordered to be pounded to death with iron pestles; but he made the speech, 'Pound, pound the pouch containing Anaxarchus; ye pound not Anaxarchus.' He had practical insight into the common illusion which identifies the ego with the self and assumes that the ego is real. He had the capacity of bringing anyone to reason in the easiest possible way. For his fortitude and contentment in life he was called the Happy Man (Diogenes Laertius 1925: 9, 58–60).

The history of scepticism is by its very nature informal and discontinuous because its practitioners did not hanker after institutional trappings or the professional status of the dogmatic sects (Annas and Barnes 1985, Hookway 1990). They depended on the example of their lives, conversation and debate for the continuation of the tradition. This contrasted with the dogmatic sects of Stoicism and Epicureanism, which were formally organized as schools and owned property. For a brief period of some two hundred years however, the Academy, founded by Plato, embraced scepticism. But then in the first century BC the sceptic Aenesidemus broke away from the Academy on the grounds that it had become dogmatically sceptical and so had betrayed the tradition.

A notable fact about Aenesidemus' successors is that many of them were physicians; in fact the physicians to the imperial household in Rome were sceptics. The last great Greek sceptic was Sextus Empiricus who was a physician and flourished in the middle of the second century AD. He wrote two works which have survived, namely the 'Outlines of Pyrrhonism' and 'Against the Mathematicians' (Sextus Empiricus 1933). 'Mathematician' is better translated 'professor' as Sextus argues against all academic philosophy rather than merely the mathematical sciences. These are our chief sources for ancient Greek scepticism and, ironically, for many of the various dogmatic schools. After Sextus Greek scepticism disappears, as it was suppressed by Christianity.

However some fourteen hundred years after Sextus' death his writings were translated and scepticism again occupied the centre of philosophical thought. In 1562, Henri Estienne, the great Renaissance printer, published a Latin edition of Sextus' work and soon all his works were published. Pyrrhonian scepticism rapidly became central to intellectual thought (Popkin 1979). Erasmus and Montaigne, scientists such as Mersenne and Gassendi, Catholic and Protestant theologians, and perhaps most important, Descartes, were all embroiled in arguments for and against scepticism. The challenge of scepticism has continued to be of great importance up to the present day.

There was in the sixteenth century one group of intellectuals who made a particularly ready and well-informed public for sceptical thought; these were physicians. Galen's works were familiar to all and they were a vast storehouse of ancient sceptical arguments. Physicians were also familiar with the Methodist way of thought which was, roughly speaking, the medical branch of Pyrrhonian scepticism.

METHODISM

Methodism arose in the reign of Tiberius at the beginning of the first century AD. Thessalos was the founder of the movement although this way of thinking could be traced back to Hippocrates and earlier (Frede 1987: 261). It was a movement of radical reform, criticizing the prevailing Rationalist and Empiricist schools for having become academic. It was called 'Methodism' because its chief concern was to answer the question 'Which is the correct method of treatment?' (cf. Galen's *De methodo medendi*). 'Method of treatment' here does not mean the way one treats a patient, but rather the way in which one arrives at a certain treatment, that is, the way one comes to think that a certain treatment is the right treatment. When this is understood it becomes clear why modern psychoanalysis, which derives from Freud and Jung, ignores scepticism, since for it this question does not arise. These analysts dogmatically assert that Freud or the founder of whatever school they belong to has stated the correct method, which is the method that his theory confirms. So a patient automatically receives the treatment that the analyst's theory indicates, and this is obtained from his own analysis and training school. There is rarely any discussion with the patient as to what is appropriate to him or her at that particular time.

Celsus, one of the early great physicians in the Methodism tradition, wrote, 'nec post rationem medicinam esse inventam; sed post inventam medicinam rationem esse quaesitam'. (The art of medicine was not a discovery following upon reasoning, but after the discovery of the remedy, the reason for it was sought (Celsus 1935).) This insight has its roots in scepticism but is ignored by some therapists, who might give treatment lasting years and claim the cure is due to the successful application of their theory. They ignore non-specific factors such as the sheer passage of time, though time is a great healer; also the fact that they have given the patient time and attention, that they have been tactful and a relatively dispassionate third party outside the patient's family and friends, all of which is likely to be of help.

The importance of these factors, rather than the popularity of any medical dogmas, was emphasized by Galen. Thus in one of his treatises on psychotherapy, he wrote that envy is the worst disease of the soul, followed by love of power and unbridled sexual lust. He noted how the upbringing of infants and children affects later life. He cured these diseases through discourse, including attention to dreams. He thought that it was the insight and attentiveness of the therapist that was important and recommended the patient choose a fearless, independent and preferably older man (we would add 'or woman') as a therapist. We must use our passions to fight our disordered passions, he thought, and he was interested in the therapeutic devices of delay and laughter (Galen 1963).

Like most ancient writers on psychotherapy Galen emphasized that what was important was the therapist's mastery of his own impulses and this included his impulse to explain and theorize. Freud was unaware that the urge to explain and theorize is by no means straightforward, a point made many times by sceptics. For ways of thinking are curiously self-authenticating. A proposition can be assessed as true or false only within a way of thinking and investigating that helps determine its truth value. What the proposition means depends on the way in which we can settle its truth. So we cannot justify any particular approach as the best way to discover the truth of the proposition, because the sense of the proposition itself depends on the way in which its truth is settled. So a way of thinking cannot be straightforwardly wrong, when it has received a status by which it fixes the sense of what it investigates, as has happened in psychoanalysis. But of course neither can it be straightforwardly right! A different way of thinking will produce different senses and truths.

If this is forgotten then psychoanalytic theory is read as if it were a direct communication of what the theorist sees to be in the mind or the unconscious; the specificity of the theorist's particular problems and approach is overlooked. His subjectivity is ignored, and this is particularly disastrous in psychotherapy, where subjectivity, the patient's uniqueness, is all important. So psychoanalysis becomes to its adherents a discourse marking some unsurpassable experience of therapy and expressing truths that are certain. So we now have dozens of different analytic therapies with their adherents but little dialogue or understanding between them. Psychoanalysts have ignored the very great influence of scepticism on science, which has shown that scientific theories are not to be adhered to uncritically, as they are not true but useful.

Thus Russell, who was influenced by the great sceptic Hume,

wrote, 'As one with a long experience of the difficulties of logic and of the deceptiveness of theories that seem irrefutable, I find myself unable to be sure of the rightness of a theory, merely on the ground that I cannot see any point on which it is wrong' (Russell 1961: 22).

Methodism flourished during the Roman empire. Perhaps the greatest exponent was Soranus, who was born in Ephesus in the middle of the first century AD, studied medicine at Alexandria and later came to Rome. His 'Gynaecology' has survived. He had a severely practical orientation, full of common sense and compassion. Like all sceptics he was familiar with the contending schools and reported their opinions with care. We must know our opponents' views as well as they do, he said. He was critical of teleology and notions of causality, both being theoretical notions; there is no ultimate cause of disease, he believed. He was attentive to the psychology of the patient. He was aware, for example, of how the feelings of the expectant mother affects the new-born baby and of how the psychological state of the woman affects whether she conceives.

To the Methodists it was the disease alone that was the teacher of what one needed to know about the treatment and so they were attentive to the varied phenomena of the disease and sceptical about all theories of aetiology involving hidden theoretical entities. The Methodists were particularly successful with chronic conditions. A modern scholar sums them up as being less pretentious, more modest, more cautious and more pragmatic than the other schools (Lloyd 1983).

As far as can now be ascertained, until present studies have borne fruit, Methodism disappeared after the fall of the Roman empire to revive again in the Renaissance. One of the last physicians to write on Methodism was Boissier de Sauvage (*Pathologia Methodica* 1752). The Methodists in these centuries were mainly concerned with boundaries and levels of description. Thus they wanted to show the limits of science in medicine. They argued that we cannot construct a concept of health from knowledge of physiology. They were well aware that the notion of health is dependent on the culture and way of life of the patient. In psychiatry they were pioneers in arguing against possession by demons. Once again these are mental entities like ego, id and superego, little persons in the inner world which are supposed to cause mental disease; we can understand the behaviour of the nuns of the Ursuline convent of Loudun better by taking account of the culture in which they lived rather than by postulating demon possession (Duncan 1634). In psychotherapy the later Methodists emphasized the importance of developing a science of signs, rather than postulating hidden theoretical mental entities, existing in themselves and causing possession. Above all, like the early Methodists, they emphasized the uniqueness of the patient and his disease and the failure of generalization to capture this.

A few themes taken from Montaigne will further illustrate the relevance of Pyrrhonian scepticism to psychotherapy.

MONTAIGNE

One of the great figures of Pyrrhonian scepticism was Montaigne. His writings are perhaps the best introduction to scepticism for psychotherapists as they are readily available in translation (Montaigne 1958, 1987 and 1991). Some of his thought is familiar from the plays of Shakespeare, who was a great admirer of his; indeed most of his last plays are meditations on sceptical themes (Cavell 1987). Montaigne's essays arose out of a crisis of melancholy brought about by the death of his closest friend and are a ruthlessly honest analysis of his own thoughts, feelings, habits and failings, written with dry humour and without jargon.

A key question here is what is meant by analysis. Montaigne's notion of what it is to analyse oneself is radically different from that of Freud, the psychoanalytic schools, and most other modern psychotherapies. In brief, Freud based his views on science and the accumulation of knowledge about the mind: science, he thought, progresses slowly but surely, since it is built on secure foundations. The rational subject is a reflective being who can stand back from engagement in the world and through reflection can come to know the objective realm of reality. In the case of the mind this is a difficult task, which primitive people, children, and neurotics cannot do; only the person analysed in the correct way can undertake it and slowly these people will build an edifice of certain knowledge of the mind. As Wallerstein recently put it, by 'cohering around our common clinical ground and by building incrementsly upon that . . . we have a firm base upon which we can painstakingly fashion a truly scientific theoretical structure' and 'we can, I am convinced, ultimately fulfil Freud's dream for the theoretical structure of the discipline and the science of psychoanalysis' (Wallerstein 1990: 11).

Montaigne, on the other hand, was not concerned to fulfil anyone's dream, but to know himself. Nor was he shackled by the ideology of the space of the clinic, where the observing look of the clinician with its logical armature is assumed to hold the key to truth, a phase of medical thought which has been well described by Foucault (1973). Montaigne wrote essays, and this is a literary term that he invented. It means a test, a try, a leap in the dark. He sought 'not to establish the truth but to seek it' (Montaigne 1957, vol. 1: 229). He did not assume that theoretical structures are the best guide to knowing oneself. He proceeded by testing things, essaying them, taking them 'from some unaccustomed point of view . . . scattering a word here, there another, samples separated from their context, dispersed, without a plan and without a promise' (ibid.: 219).

He made no claim to being an expert who had mastered himself: 'The more I frequent myself and know myself, the more my deformity astonishes me, and the less I understand myself' (Montaigne 1957, vol. 3: 787). He was not a dispassionate observer of himself but he attended to himself: 'if others examined themselves attentively, as I do, they would find themselves, as I do, full of inanity and nonsense. Get rid of it I cannot without getting rid of myself' (ibid.: 766).

Montaigne liked to emphasize the importance of forgetting and rather boasted about his poor memory: 'excellent memories are prone to be joined to feeble judgements' (Montaigne 1957, vol. 1: 22). He said that what is important is to know oneself and this does not involve remembering facts about oneself. Each instant is a beginning, it causes us to be reborn both for ourselves and to the world. When he complains about his lack of memory he is calling attention to the perpetual forgetting that is the counterpart to spontaneity. He sometimes characterizes his thought as a dream or reverie.

Scepticism is a movement in which we reject the seductive illusions of life and at the same time realize that there is no pure place from which we can observe the world objectively. This is in marked contrast to Freud, who was sceptical about what his patients said but had an almost mystical belief in the objectivity of science and his own interpretations. Montaigne was acutely aware, like all sceptics, that the world is mostly lies and treachery: 'Dissimulation is among the most notable qualities of this century . . . Deceit maintains and feeds most of men's occupations' (Montaigne 1957, vol. 3: 604). Yet on the other hand, 'Dreams are faithful interpreters of our inclinations . . . there is an art to sorting and understanding them' (ibid.: 843).

> Sleeping we are awake, and waking asleep. I do not see so clearly in sleep; but my wakefulness I never find pure and cloudless enough. Moreover sleep in its depth sometimes puts dreams to sleep. But

our wakefulness is never so awake as to purge and properly dissip-
ate reveries, which are the dreams of the waking, and worse than
dreams.

(Montaigne 1957, vol. 2: 451)

Some of this is reminiscent of Bion (1970) who wrote of the
importance of eschewing memory and desire in psychoanalysis; for
memory and desire are possessions and the patient may feel this and
so become dominated by the feeling that he is possessed by and
contained in the analyst's state of mind. However Bion sees the
suppression of memory and desire as a technical procedure that the
analyst must deliberately impose on himself. Montaigne, on the other
hand, shuns all artificial procedures; only what he finds out in the
course of his 'essays' is worth while, for these truths are written in our
nerves and muscles. So he is critical of intellectuals because they are
only concerned to know about other people, being careful to distinguish themselves from the object of their knowledge – a primary
aim of psychoanalysis. Montaigne thought that one must become one
and the same with what one knows, which of course is not the same as
identifying with it. The best evidence for this knowledge are one's
actions. Life is good for those who rely on practical wisdom, 'a
wisdom not so ingenious, robust, and pompous as that of [the
psychologists'] invention, but correspondingly easy and salutary,
performing very well what the other talks about' (Montaigne 1957:
vol. 3: 822).

It is in the ordinary use of language that Montaigne seeks to find
himself: 'each man is in some sort in his work' (Montaigne 1957, vol.
2: 279). It is not by creating a technical vocabulary which is supposed
to be a true description of the processes of the mind that he reveals
himself but in the way he *uses* language:

Handling and use by able minds give value to a language, not so
much by innovating as by filling it out with more vigorous and
varied services, by stretching and bending it. They do not bring to
it new words, but they enrich their own, give more weight and
depth to their meaning and use; they teach the language unaccustomed movements, but prudently and shrewdly.

(Montaigne 1957, vol. 3: 665)

He plays with language and allows language to play him. It is through
our mother tongue that we can come to understand ourselves better.

This is in complete contrast to the psychoanalytic use of language.

Psychoanalysts claim to be experts in one area of the mind, the unconscious. So they have developed a special language to describe the
processes they observe within it, just like an engineer who uses a
special language to describe the workings of a machine. Unfor-
tunately, as mental processes are fictions of the imagination, different
schools of psychoanalysis describe different processes. So we now have
a plethora of technical languages; we have dictionaries for Freudian,
Jungian, Kleinian, and no doubt other schools for psychotherapy.
Thus dialogue between psychotherapists is effectively blocked and the
monological character of psychoanalysis confirmed.

The technical language of the various schools is best understood as
strings of slogans. A slogan is produced collectively, it is a collective
formulation within a group, generally an institutional one. A slogan
is not a personal truth, an expression of what *you* mean to say to a
particular person but is judged by the group as being correct or not;
students have to learn when it is correct to use a particular slogan and
when not. What is important is not that the slogan is true, but that it
is correct. Its purpose is not to provide a representation of parts of a
mechanism, as do technical languages, but to name and produce an
effect, that is, to produce solidarity in the school and to sound clever
and scientific. There is no evidence that the use of particular slogans
aids the understanding and relief of mental pain and suffering in any
deep sense. This contrasts with the necessity for a surgeon to understand the technical language naming the parts of the body he under-
takes to mend. Montaigne considered universities to be 'talking-
shops' (*escoles de la parlerie*). Perhaps the same could be said of schools
for psychotherapy.

It should be pointed out that Montaigne was not an eccentric
pedant, the usual picture that analysts have of a philosopher, but a
man steeped in traditional thought who lived as he thought. He was
twice mayor of Bordeaux, in those days a very powerful and difficult
position to hold and he eventually became a friend and adviser to the
king of France and was respected throughout Europe. He was an
outspoken critic of the Inquisition, then a dangerous position to take
up. Man's false opinion of knowledge and its value, the vanity and
presumption that results – these were his targets. 'It is an absolute
perfection and virtually divine to know how to enjoy our being right-
fully', he wrote (Montaigne 1957: vol. 3: 857); and this is a matter of
reason and judgement rather than accumulating knowledge and
applying theories. So to him 'primitive people' may well have been
more reasonable than we are, for they judged rightly the importance

of being close to nature and their mother tongue, they had the candour that he strove for and that most of us have lost. There is no progress in being human.

THE PERSON AND THE SELF

'Authors communicate with the people by some special extrinsic mark, I am the first to do so by my entire being, as Michel de Montaigne, not as a grammarian or a poet or a jurist' (Montaigne 1957, 3, 2: 611). This statement sums up the critical difference between a psychotherapy true to the insights of Pyrrhonian scepticism and one based on the metaphysical beliefs basic to the enterprise of the Enlightenment. Believers in the latter 'observe' what they imagine to be the mind, the self, the inner world, or behaviour and try to make a special science from their 'observations' and inferences; this science, they believe, will enable us gradually to close the gaps in our knowledge and conquer disease and unhappiness.

Pyrrhonian scepticism, on the other hand, is an ability to suspend beliefs and the assertions of knowledge based upon them. It is alert to the dangers of reifying and so building knowledge upon imaginative pictures of the mind, such as were created by Freud and elaborated by his followers. Self-knowledge requires vigilant attention to our natural spontaneity. 'If each man watched closely the effects and circumstances of the passions that dominate him, as I have done with the ones I have fallen prey to, he would see them coming and would check their impetuosity and course a bit' (Montaigne 1957, 3, 13: 822). But of course this contains a paradox: if we try to become sincere then we falsify ourselves and create beliefs about ourselves; we alter ourselves in the very attempt to portray ourselves. Our being is 'complete' only at the moment it becomes ambiguous, that is, only at the moment when, taking form in language, it becomes suspicious of betraying its true identity. The naming and predictive power of language must be suspended to make room for the reality of the subject.

This results in a sort of circular movement characteristic of Pyrrhonian writing and practice:

The range of our desires should be circumscribed and restrained to a narrow limit of the nearest and most contiguous good things; and moreover their course should be directed not in a straight line that ends up elsewhere, but in a circle whose two extremities by a short sweep meet and terminate in ourselves. Actions that are performed without this reflexive movement, I mean a searching and genuine reflexive movement – the actions, for example of the avaricious, the ambitious, and so many others who run in a straight line, whose course carries them forward – are erroneous and diseased actions.

(Montaigne 1957, 3, 10: 773)

This circular movement which makes room for the reality of the subject is nothing to do with the development of an inner self or the strengthening of the ego or the enriching of the inner world. All these are myths built on blind adherence to mixtures of Cartesian rationalism and British empiricism (Kenny 1989). They never make precise the relationship between a person and his or her self, ego, or inner world. They hover between saying that people *have* selves and that they *are* selves. In either case it is clear that the self is not a tangible body of flesh and blood. At best the self merely refers to the elements of human life that are private to the person, his secret thoughts and ambitions. But what is really significant is the person's actual 'essays' in the public world; here inner entities are not in play but the man of flesh and blood is: 'Michel de Montaigne'.

CONCLUSION

About a hundred years after the death of Montaigne Pyrrhonian scepticism became less prominent and arguments about Cartesian scepticism became important. Descartes claimed to extend sceptical doubt as far as it could be taken, in order to find a foundation to knowledge which was resistant to doubt. He found this in the Cogito. He could not doubt his own existence or that he is a being that thinks. This led him to a dualism of mind and body which comprised two distinct substances. He held that man's essence is mind, and the essence of mind is consciousness, for that is what we are most certain of.

This picture of the mind inspired thinkers of the Enlightenment and continued in one form or another into this century. Freud took it for granted. He thought that consciousness makes us aware only of our own states of mind. We have to infer that other people possess consciousness as we have to infer that unconscious processes occur in us (Freud 1984: 170). The problem for neurotics, psychotics, and for normal human development, as Freud saw it, is how can we get from the inner world, subject to pleasure, to the outer 'real' world: a typically Cartesian approach to the relation of the mind to the world.

The scepticism that Descartes encouraged was inimical to the original aim of Pyrrhonian scepticism which was peace of mind through the cure of conflict. Scepticism became of academic import-ance only, a point highlighted by Hume who wrote that scepticism 'overheats the brain', so 'I am ready to reject all belief and reasoning, and can look upon no opinion even as more probable or likely than another.' Fortunately nature comes to the rescue

> and cures me of this philosophical melancholy and delirium . . . I dine, I play a game of back-gammon, I converse, and am merry with my friends; and when after three or four hours' amusement, I wou'd return to these speculations, they appear so cold and strain'd, and ridiculous, that I cannot find in my heart to enter into them any farther.
>
> (Hume 1978: 268–9)

Psychoanalysis too has a similar conflict. Freud and most analysts prefer to see themselves as scientists who are gradually plotting out the structure of the mind. Psychotherapists who simply try to help people to resolve their conflicts and do not follow a theory are a lowly breed. On the other hand most patients seek help and are not so interested in the austere position of being an object for observation.

It is the work of Wittgenstein that is mainly responsible for the renewed interest in Pyrrhonian scepticism in the latter half of this century (Fogelin 1987: 226). He saw philosophy as being primarily therapeutic. 'Philosophy is a battle against the bewitchment of our intelligence by means of language' (Wittgenstein 1958: para. 109). We readily live by false beliefs about the nature of the human subject, the 'I', 'self-knowledge', rules, thinking, imagining and so on, and these lead to confusions, conflict, and mental pain; think for example of the dogmatism with which a depressed person holds on to certain beliefs about himself. Wittgenstein's scepticism is not directed at the everyday background of our lives, our human form of life, but at how our lives become twisted so that we hang on dogmatically to beliefs.

As Sextus Empricus put it over two thousand years ago, the Pyrrhonist is 'a lover of his kind' who desires to 'cure by speech, as best he can, the self-conceit and rashness of the Dogmatists' (Sextus Empiricus 1933: Bk 3, Ch. 33).

REFERENCES

Annas, J. and Barnes, J. (1985) *The Modes of Scepticism*, Cambridge: Cambridge University Press.

Anzieu, D. (1986) *Freud's Self-Analysis*, London: Hogarth Press.

Bion, W. R. (1970) *Attention and Interpretation*, London: Tavistock Publications.

Cavell, S. (1987) *Disowning Knowledge in Six Plays of Shakespeare*, Cambridge: Cambridge University Press.

Celsus (1935) *de Medecina*, vol. 1, *Prooemium*, trans. W. G. Spencer, Loeb Classical Library, London: Heinemann.

Diogenes Laertius (1925) *Lives of Eminent Philosophers*, trans. R. D. Hicks, Loeb Classical Library, London: Heinemann.

Duncan, Mark (1634) *Discours de la possession des religieuses de Loudin*, Saumer.

Editorial (1984) *The Journal of the Melanie Klein Society* 2 (2).

Fogelin, R. J. (1987) *Wittgenstein*, London: Routledge & Kegan Paul.

Foucault, M. (1973) *The Birth of the Clinic*, trans. A. M. Sheridan Smith, London: Tavistock Publications.

Frede, M. (1987) *Essays in Ancient Philosophy*, Oxford: Clarendon Press.

Freud, E. L. (ed.) (1961) *Letters of Sigmund Freud, 1873-1939*, trans. T. and J. Stern, London: Hogarth Press.

Freud, S. (1926) 'The question of lay analysis', *Standard Edition of the Complete Psychological Works of Sigmund Freud*, 24 vols, 1953-74, edited by J. Strachey, London: Hogarth Press (SE) 20.

—— (1933) *New Introductory Lectures on Psycho-Analysis* SE 22.

—— (1973) *Introductory Lectures on Psychoanalysis*, vol. 1, Harmondsworth: Penguin Books.

—— (1984) *On Metapsychology: the Theory of Psychoanalysis*, Harmondsworth: Penguin Books.

Galen (1821-33) *De methodo medendi*, vol. 10, ed. K. G. Kühn, Leipzig.

—— (1963) *Galen on the Passions and Errors of the Soul*, trans. P. W. Hawkins, Columbus, Ohio: Ohio State University Press.

Hacking, I. (1990) *The Taming of Chance*, Cambridge: Cambridge University Press.

Hegel, G. W. F. (1975) *Aesthetics*, trans. T. M. Knox, vol. 1, Oxford: Clarendon Press.

Hookway, C. (1990) *Scepticism*, London: Routledge.

Hume, D. (1978) *A Treatise of Human Nature*, Oxford: Clarendon Press.

Kant, I. (1957) *The Critique of Judgement*, trans. J. C. Meredeth, Oxford: Clarendon Press.

Kenny, A. (1989) *The Metaphysics of Mind*, Oxford: Clarendon Press.

Lloyd, G. E. R. (1983) *Science, Folklore and Ideology: Studies in the Life Sciences in Ancient Greece*, Cambridge: Cambridge University Press.

Masson, J. F. (ed.) (1985) *The Complete Letters of Sigmund Freud to Wilhelm Fliess 1887-1904*, trans. J. F. Masson, Cambridge, Mass.: Harvard University Press.

Montaigne, M. de (1957) *The Complete Works of Montaigne*, trans. D. M. Frame, Stanford, Calif.: Stanford University Press.

—— (1958) *Essays*, trans. J. M. Cohen, Harmondsworth: Penguin Books.

—— (1987) *An Apology for Raymond Sebond*, trans. M. A. Screech, Harmondsworth: Penguin Books.

—— (1991) *The Complete Essays*, trans. M. A. Screech, Harmondsworth: Penguin Books.

Needham, R. (1981) *Circumstantial Deliveries*, Berkeley, Calif.: University of California Press.

Popkin, R. H. (1979) *The History of Scepticism from Erasmus to Spinoza*, Berkeley, Calif.: University of California Press.

Russell, B. (1961) *Introduction to Tractatus Logico-Philosophicus, by L. Wittgenstein*, London: Routledge & Kegan Paul.

Sahlins, M. (1987) *Islands of History*, London: Tavistock Publications.

Sauvage, Boissier de (1752) *Pathologia Methodica*, Amsterdam.

Sextus Empiricus (1933) *Outlines of Pyrrhonism*, trans. R. G. Bury, Loeb Classical Library, London: Heinemann.

Wallerstein, R. S. (1990) 'Psychoanalysis: the common ground', *International Journal of Psychoanalysis* 71(3): 3–20.

Wittgenstein, L. (1958) *Philosophical Investigations*, trans. G. E. M. Anscombe, Oxford: Blackwell.

Wordsworth, W. (1964) *The Prelude: Essay, Supplementary to the Preface*, ed. E. de Selincourt, London: Oxford University Press.

Chapter 6

Tradition, violence and psychotherapy

Zbigniew Kotowicz

> History is hysterical: it is constituted only if we consider it, only if we look at it – and in order to look at it, we must be excluded from it. As a living soul I am the very contrary of History, I am what belies it, destroys it for the sake of my own history.
>
> (Roland Barthes, *Camera Lucida*)

> People who cannot find their way out of history are lost.
>
> (Elias Canetti, *The Human Province*)

I

A man in his mid-twenties is seeing a psychotherapist. One day he arrives for a session and begins by saying, 'Last night I couldn't sleep, it was going around my head that my girl-friend was going to be killed in a car accident.' The therapist has known the man for about a year. He has frequent panic attacks, he feels unable to join crowds, he is preoccupied with death. But what he is saying now is a little different; it seems to come out of the blue, there is something odd about it and it is difficult to make much sense of it. The man had never before spoken about his girl-friend in a charged manner and suddenly he says this: for no clear reason he fears she is going to be killed in a car accident. What does it mean? The therapist looks over some well-worn blueprints. Perhaps some concealed hostility towards the girl-friend is coming to light? No. Perhaps it is a case of displacement, that is, it has nothing to do with the girl-friend but expresses a fear or hostility towards someone else? It does not seem so. The denials are real; these interpretations do not make sense, they are simply not true. The therapist draws a blank. But the man remains tense, almost agitated. He tries to dismiss the story as trivial and irrelevant but he does not succeed. It is clear that is not meaningless.

As the conversation meanders on the therapist remembers that the man's uncle was killed in some accident. He asks, and the man confirms, yes, his uncle, and also his grandmother and another uncle. Three deaths in three separate accidents. Two killed by a train, one by a car. It all happened a long time ago. His father was then a young man but already married with children and suddenly he lost in quick succession, and all in tragic circumstances, his mother and two brothers. After this series of deaths he suffered a bout of depression and he consulted his doctor. The doctor came up with a remedy: the young man should have another child, that will take his mind off his worries. He followed the doctor's advice, another child was born and indeed his depression went away (more or less). This third child, a son, the cure for the father's depression, grew up to be the man with panic attacks, with a fear of death, with the inexplicable conviction that his girl-friend will be killed in a car accident. He was born to carry his father's fears. His place was marked.

The dynamics of the relationship that develop between the father and the son have their contour outlined in advance, before the game is enacted. They were written up by the circumstances which led to the conception. And so the place that the young man occupies in his father's life shapes his relationship with him. The father loves him, this son even seems to be his favourite. He is in general very helpful and supportive, but with one notable exception. Though a cultured and educated man he cannot, for some unfathomable reason, tolerate that his son wants to be a painter. This peculiarity confirms what role his son is meant to play in his life. Those killed in the accidents were the artists in the family. His son's artistic leanings remind the father of the dead and this he must not do; he exists in order to make oblivion possible. He occupies a place which is in the shadow of death and his father attempts to prevent him from bringing it to life. All he can do is to carry it silently.

That place which is assigned to the new-born is like a chrysalis destined to become identity. Relation to parents, siblings, class, race, nationality – these are like cards dealt for the game of life to be played. Sometimes – and this is what the therapist faces – the hand seems unplayable, there is a malignant joker in the pack. Hidden, it can override anything, render projects untenable, wreak havoc. It can come up at any time, always the same, without any reference to context. Repetition.

The young man has panic attacks, he enacts repetitively what his father wants to forget. Freud was intrigued by the phenomenon of repetition. At first he thought it to be a pleasure-seeking mechanism. But he learnt that there were people constantly reliving scenes in their dreams, such as war traumas, which could not possibly be interpreted as pleasant. Realizing that it is not the pursuit of pleasure which institutes repetition he embarks on a powerful speculative meditation and he formulates the concept of the death drive. Freud has it that death is an instinctual affair, that humans have a regressive drive, which like a biological force pulls them towards death. Repetition of unpleasant situations is the enactment of the most archaic part of the inner self, it is the pulse of the death drive. The concept of the death instinct closes Freud's speculative system and turns it into a teleology. '*The aim of all life is death*' (Freud 1920: 38). Freud felt this statement to be sufficiently important to italicize it. It is a peculiar teleology. This death which is life's aim does not finalize and crown life but is a regression, a moving back to the pre-organic state of matter from which it first rose. From ashes to ashes. Death is from the very beginning undoing life. One should note that at first glance a metaphysical improbability seems to be presenting itself. It is clear that to Freud life is something contingent, liable to happen but not necessary. Death, on the other hand, is a necessity. A metaphysician would wonder how could the contingent (life) give rise to the necessary (death). He (the metaphysician) would find such a proposition unacceptable and in order to solve this problem he would no doubt introduce into the equation some form of the absolute (God, Spirit). But this is not necessary. Freud inverts the proposition, he states that death precedes life: '*inaninmate things existed before living ones*' (1920: 38). By dying we move back towards that which already exists, into a non-being which Freud, ever attached to biological imagery, terms the 'pre-organic state'. So how would life (the contingent) emerge from death (the necessary)? Well, it does not really, because what 'would thus present us to-day with the picture of phenomena of life', are in fact 'circuitous paths to death' (1920: 39). And if we think that we witness a full variety of life which, for all the threats, still seems inextinguishable, Freud retorts that what we take to be the abundance of life is nothing else but the simple fact that every 'organism wishes to die in its own fashion'. Would this then mean that, after all, in wishing to die in its own fashion, the organism has something like life-preserving instincts which are genuinely independent of death? Not quite, as 'these guardians of life, too, were originally the myrmidions of death',

(1920: 39). So why is there life? It is because death invents phenomena of life to act itself out, because death likes to repeat itself. So while in its insistence to arrive at the point of death an individual organism is teleological, death itself is not. It has no master, it serves no Absolute which would give it meaning. It is utterly aimless, all it wants to do is to repeat itself, and that is why it keeps on inventing life. So though the aim of all life is death, this aim is utterly aimless. This is a genuinely radical nihilism.

But the death that haunts the man who consulted the psychotherapist has nothing metaphysical or instinctual about it. It does indeed, as Freud postulated, precede his life, but it is not 'in him', instinctually or otherwise. It is 'outside' just like Oedipus' curse. Oedipus was born into it, his fate was pronounced before he was conceived. It was his father Laius who brought upon himself the curse by raping his best friend's son.

*   *   *

Someone haunted by a fear of death, bombarded with strange thoughts, experiencing difficulties which do not seem of his or her making, and who feels denied the right to live a kind of life that he or she would want, will seek help and consult a psychotherapist. And who is the psychotherapist who offers help? It is someone who is trained to do the job, someone who is handed over the necessary knowledge to do it. One can only be a psychotherapist if one has been subjected to a hand-over. In psychoanalysis, and the groups that model themselves on it, the process of hand-over is strict. Years of personal analysis are followed by years of work under supervision and a good comprehension of theoretical knowledge is needed. It is all done in the name of thoroughness and rigour. But psychoanalysis is also a doctrine with a well-established belief system to which psychoanalysts should adhere. The hand-over is not only in the sphere of know-how, its other aim is to preserve the doctrine.

A doctrine is organized around two principal features. First there is the fundamental Truth around which the doctrine evolves. This often comes to the founder of the doctrine in the form of a revelation, and such was the case with Freud. He first communicated it in a letter to his friend Fliess: 'One thought of general value has been *revealed* to me. I have found, in my own case too, falling in love with the mother and jealousy of the father, and I now regard it as a *universal* event of early childhood' (1897: 265, italics added). Very swiftly, a single thought is instantly regarded as a universal event. This is not some timid speculative hypothesis, this is the real stuff of a Revelation. Freud had the Word. In fact, it was no doubt Freud's personal experience, most likely disconcerting, but he declares its 'general value' and then he can say, 'in my own case *too*'. He sets out to turn the revelation into a doctrine. To his followers it becomes an article of faith. The first disciples were expected to accept more or less unconditionally Freud's teachings on childhood sexuality.[1]

The second important feature in the formation of a doctrine is the unquestioning reverence and loyalty to the founder who had the revelation, in this instance, to Freud. He was no ordinary man. He was a genius, courageous and unique. He was the master who accomplished a feat which was nothing short of superhuman and heroic. European culture has produced only a few who are equal to him.[2] Perhaps Freud would not go along with such extravagant veneration but nevertheless he did see himself on a mission to teach humanity the truth. And every mission needs missionaries. The conditions of acceptance were severe. Freud demanded that his followers abandon their careers and give themselves unquestioningly to the new doctrine. The missionary should believe the cause and revere the founding master. What follows is the very intense relationship of the master and the disciple. The new adept is claimed by Freud and the cause to the extent that his individuality is at stake. One account of the nature of the discipleship in psychoanalysis goes so far as to suggest that the personality of the therapist is filled out with that of the master and the doctrine to such an extent that it has a psychotic element to it.[3]

What one can observe here is a formation of a group which is bound together in such a way that one has to call it a sect (from *sequi*, to follow). A sect forms its own tradition. The term 'tradition' has many meanings in everyday use. It may mean heritage, a general feeling of history. It may mean custom. We speak of the family tradition, or of tradition in art; folk music is sometimes referred to as traditional music. It seems that anything which is in one way or another related to the past can be referred to as traditional. But in one context it has a very specific meaning. The word has its root in the Latin *tradere*, to hand over. The French derive *traduire*, to translate, from it. The same root lies behind the words 'treason' and 'betrayal'. These different meanings springing from the same root are not just an etymological curiosity. The double-edged meaning of the hand-over goes back to the early days of Christianity, to the time of the Roman persecutions. A new disciple to the faith was handed over the gospels with a clear brief: he was to find new disciples to teach the revelation and he was forbidden to let the gospels pass over to the enemies. If under the pressure of persecution a disciple handed over the gospels to the Romans he became a traitor. He was expelled from the Church; he no longer belonged to the tradition. This ambivalent significance of the handing over gives the notion of tradition a very specific meaning. To belong to the tradition one has to be true to the Word that is transmitted; one must not hand it over to the enemy, if he exists; and one must teach it faithfully. Only in Latin and the languages which take their vocabulary from it do the words 'tradition' and 'betrayal' share an etymological root. This linkage is peculiar to the mechanics of the formation of a new doctrine. It is in this sense that tradition is most clearly articulated in psychoanalysis. It is no coincidence that Lacan referrred to his expulsion from the International Psychoanalytical Association as excommunication. Psychoanalysis trades in truth, it establishes lines of loyalty, it out-lines rules of who is in, who is out. A sect always entails a 'we', it is a mark of hostility. It is a game of followers, successions, heretics, schisms, expulsions.

In *Moses and Monotheism* Freud theorizes that at the origins of a people as a definable group with its own religion, culture and so on, lies the killing of the founding father. This prehistoric act is repeated over and over again. Each beginning commences with parricide. It is diffi-cult to see how one could sustain Freud's argument on a scale that he seemed to envisage. Parricide at the beginning of every culture? The Eskimos, the Vikings? But perhaps Freud's speculation is truer to the origins of a tradition. If that is so, and since it appears that psycho-analysis is striving to create its own tradition, then one would expect to find parricide at the beginnings of psychoanalysis. And one need not look far: the killed father is Breuer.

The chronological table of Freud's life and intellectual develop-ment which we find in the Penguin edition of Freud's works has a few entries directly concerning Breuer.

*c.*1888   [Freud] begins to follow Breuer in using hypnosis for cathartic treatment of hysteria
1893   Publication of Breuer and Freud, 'Preliminary Communica-tion: exposition of trauma theory of hysteria and of cathartic treatment'
1895   Jointly with Breuer, *Studies on Hysteria*
1893–6 Gradual divergence of views between Freud and Breuer

Behind these dry phrases lies a complex story. Breuer, fourteen years older than Freud and a well-established psychiatrist in Vienna, was a mentor and supporter (also a financial one) of the then struggling Freud. Freud's attachment to him was great, and he named his first daughter Mathilde in honour of Breuer's wife. There is no doubt that the years of work with Breuer were of critical importance to Freud's development and that it was then that he was set on the path that led to psychoanalysis.

In 1910, almost fifteen years after the end of the collaboration between Freud and Breuer, Freud was invited to Clark University in the United States to present his new theory. This, 'Five lectures on psychoanalysis', is the first of the several accounts of psychoanalysis that he was to give over the years. After the opening 'Ladies and gentlemen . . .' he begins with the following:

> If it is a merit to have brought psychoanalysis into being, that merit is not mine. I had no share in its earliest beginnings. I was a student and working for my final examination at the time when another Viennese physician, Dr. Josef Breuer first (in 1880–82) made use of this procedure . . .
>
> (Freud 1910: 9)

So it was Breuer who brought psychoanalysis into being; he was its real father.

Four years later, in *On the History of the Psychoanalytic Movement*, the tone is altogether different. Freud wrote this account of psychoanalysis in response to the defections of Adler and Jung from the camp. But his attitude to Breuer has also changed. He states that some 'well-disposed persons' were of the opinion that in the Clark University lectures he had exaggerated Breuer's importance. And Freud thinks they were right. Breuer's contribution to the development of the theory was in fact minimal; all the ground-breaking discoveries were Freud's alone. And he produces what he considers a decisive argument as to why Breuer should not be accorded any position in the history of the movement: unlike Freud and his early followers Breuer never suffered the criticism and abuse that psychoanalysis provoked. This is a sound religious argument: only martyrdom secures a place in tradition.

In 1880, before the two met, Breuer treated a very disturbed woman. Fifteen years later, at Freud's instigation, he recounted the work in *Studies on Hysteria* as the case of Anna O. In the Clark University lectures Freud refers to this case as the first in which the psychoanalytical procedure was employed. But later things change. The denigration of the case of Anna O becomes part of the slaying of Breuer. In the English translation of the case of Anna O we find a footnote which explains the story. It is worth quoting in full:

> At this point (so Freud once told the present translator, with his finger on an open copy of the book) there is a hiatus in the text. What he had in mind and went on to describe was the occurrence which marked the end of Anna O's treatment. The whole story is told by Ernest Jones in his life of Freud, and it is enough to say here that when the treatment had apparently reached a successful end, the patient suddenly made manifest to Breuer the presence of a strong unanalysed positive transference of an unmistakably sexual nature. It was this occurrence, Freud believed, that caused Breuer to hold back the publication of the case history for so many years and that led ultimately to his abandonment of all further collaboration in Freud's researches.
>
> (Freud 1895: 40–1)

One wonders if there is a term for the operation of filling out, without the author's consent, a 'hiatus in the text'. It is something like inverted censorship; whereas the censor deletes, here it is the case of adding to the text. At any rate, this kind of a footnote from a translator is nothing else but a gross violation, an interference with the writing. This rather crude tactic has a clear aim; it is done in order to impress upon the reader the worthlessness of Breuer's work. According to Ernest Jones, one of Freud's most trusty lieutenants, Breuer was so terrified of Anna O's sexual transference that he ran away with his wife on a second honeymoon. On the few occasions when Freud himself mentioned the matter in writing he never claimed to know this to be a fact. This is how he says he *interprets* the reason Breuer finished treatment. At least one historian checked all the facts and dates of Jones's account and doubts it (Ellenberger 1970: 483–4). But most have swallowed it hook, line and sinker. It is worth noting that the actual facts of the case as recounted by Breuer were never disputed. And it is a quite remarkable story, both as far as the range of symptoms that Anna O exhibited is concerned, and Breuer's work with her. His account is entirely free from any speculation, and he claimed his work to have been a success. Anna O was in real life Bertha Pappenheim, a woman who later, after the period described by Breuer, achieved considerable reputation for her work as a social worker and defender of women's rights. Whether her apparent change was due to Breuer's work has been disputed (as one would expect), but still, this is one of the most interesting cases that we find in the Collected Works of Sigmund Freud. But it was not Freud's case.

What was Breuer's crime? It had little to do with Anna O. Though well disposed towards Freud and his work, Breuer did not accept the early teachings about childhood sexuality. He did not believe in the revelation. Therefore, he was a traitor. A father is slain, a new tradition is born.

*   *   *

The young man who wants to be a painter is preoccupied with death. Why? Because he exists in order that his father can forget it. The father handed over the fear of death. He has a depression, a new child is born and the depression is handed over. Such is also the story of Oedipus who is handed over the curse incurred by his father's transgression. But a hand-over in the family is rarely as clear-cut as this. It is more complex, more like a whole tissue than a single traceable event. Nevertheless, it has certain characteristics. Strictly speaking one cannot say that it is 'inside' the person nor can one say that it is 'outside'. It is between, a passage from one to another, from one generation to the next. Even if it is a single event which determines the shape of the hand-over (a father's depression, a mother's madness, Laius' transgression) it is not reducible to this one event. It constitutes a line, a path, which the individual will or will not, as the case may be, follow. This hand-over may also turn into a rigid intransigent identity, not subject to any external influence or the passage of time, it becomes fate. This intransigence, incidentally, is very much how Freud characterized the unconscious. How does this happen? The principal condition is that the hand-over is hidden. It is an identity wrapped up in silence. Poor Oedipus was never told who his father was.

Families develop into lines and dynasties. The rises, the falls, and the ends are chains of hand-overs. The Oedipus legend is part of the rise and fall of the house of Labdacus, the conception and final destruction of Thebes. Viewed diachronically the individual's life is like an entry in a multi-volume family saga, volume six, chapter four. Chapter after chapter the whole saga unfolds. It may even appear to have an internal logic. But although both in families and sects one can see the process of a hand-over there are fundamental differences between them.

A sect needs to define itself. It is precise about its articles of faith, it attends to problems of hierarchy with utmost care. Its existence depends on being able to maintain a high level of homogeneity. The game of the family is not so straightforward. The primary component of a family is kinship. Kinship is a fact, and it is immutable. Perhaps the only thing that is common to all families is that they evolve around kinship. But kinship cannot be simultaneous with law. To claim that it is, that the fact of being born and having parents, grandparents and some other relations carries with it a set of prescriptions and obligations about family life is to claim that a 'what is' has inscribed in it an 'ought to'. This has been frequently done, and was done by Freud, but philosophers from Hume and Kant to Wittgenstein and Lyotard have repeatedly shown that deriving prescriptions from statements of fact is not a legitimate move. Families develop customs, laws and their mythologies, but they are subject to change. If they fossilize into a sectarian shape they breed violence and illness, as every family therapist will confirm. And while families know every form of violence, including killing, it is significant that expulsion is extremely rare, and when it happens it is usually done on religious grounds.[4] Strictly speaking, an absolute expulsion is not possible as this would mean a dissolution of kinship, and this no law can do. In the final analysis one will probably find that, for better or worse, families are essentially unruly and anarchic. There is no revealed truth to hold a family together, it is never clear what is going to be handed over, who is going to hand over, and in what manner it will be done. It is hard to see how it could be shown that the Oedipus complex, or 'the law of the father' are inherent in the family bonding.

These few sketchy remarks obviously do not exhaust the topic, they simply aim to suggest that although a family may sometimes resemble a sect and a sect may aspire to be like a family (with 'brothers', 'sisters' etc.) they are essentially different phenomena. It would then follow that problems that are generated by a family are different from those that arise in a sect. The family does not have strictly defined boundaries and it cannot be closed into any permanent system. The more open and welcoming the family, the healthier it is. A sect thrives on closedness.

*   *   *

A patient meets the analyst in the consulting room. It is said that this situation triggers off in both of them the same type of unconscious material, known as transference and countertransference. Although the psychoanalyst is meant to be less affected by transference than the patient, the difference is only quantitive. Transference and countertransference are posited as a symmetry. But the analytical encounter involves also another interchange, which creates a fundamental asymmetry between the patient and the analyst. What makes someone a patient (in this context)[5] is the conflict with his kin. The patient comes from the chaos of a family. He is at a moment of transition, from the identity which has been handed over to him to something which is still unknown. He is in a way bound by the edict, 'Honour your father and your mother'. It paralyses, because 'to honour' has been transformed into the command 'Obey'. He does not want to accept the hand-over and this comes across as an act of disobedience.

The analyst bears opposite hallmarks. He adheres to a doctrine, and is likely to harbour illusions of already knowing what the answers are even if humbly acknowledging that he has not yet fully mastered the truth. He is in no form of transition, he has a faith which he is ready to hand over. The psychotherapist belongs whereas the patient feels exiled. It is like an encounter between a newly born Christian and a lost Jew. Out of this asymmetry three basic permutations occur.

1 The patient accepts the ideology of the analyst and moves from the uncertainty of the disintegrating family identity to the ready-made doctrine. He is converted. In some cases he may decide to become a missionary himself and he enters psychoanalytical training.
2 The patient does not accept the ideology and the analyst offers no alternative. The result is chronic stalemate.
3 The analyst suspends the doctrine and leaves the space open.

II

At its most orthodox the psychoanalytical discourse presents itself as an unbreakable monolith. The theory is tight, it can explain all shades and nuances of human behaviour. It is a single-cause theory, everything a variation on one basic mechanism, be it the Oedipus complex, or splitting between the good and bad breast. The theory acts like a catch-all net, and the therapeutic attitude reflects the theory. In the extreme cases the therapist is an interpreting machine 'applying' the theory to practice. In such an instance, and it does happen, the patient is effectively terrorized by the theory of the analyst. Freud himself was not always as consistent as his writings suggest. In his consulting room he often deviated from the procedures he himself recommended. And many therapists still do. They show emotions, they worry about their patients, they lose their tempers, in short, they often act in ways which would not be considered appropriate to the high standards that the

the profession demands. But they tend to admit to it only in private.

However, there are some notable exceptions. One who stands out is D. W. Winnicott. By looking at certain things he has to say one can begin to examine in some detail issues involved in the suspending of doctrine in psychoanalytical work. Winnicott is an interesting figure because on the one hand his development took place within the psychoanalytical domain and he always remained in it, while on the other hand he developed ideas which run counter to the most basic assumptions of the doctrine. At some points his thinking challenges the theoretical and therapeutic dogma alike.

To begin with Winnicott had a certain basic attitude, a general conviction about what the humans are, that was different from Freud's. Freud was a master of suspicion, a profound pessimist who did not believe in genuine happiness and well-being. He thought man to be in essence a savage whose real yearnings are unacceptable to the norms of the society, or, putting it in Freud's own terms, the pleasure principle is kept in check by the reality principle. Out of this basic condition the human struggles to carve out a reasonable existence. He may engage in all sorts of enterprises, write poetry or paint, be religious, work, fall in love, make friends, but somehow, all these are only a myriad of illusions, subliminal guises, acted out homosexuality, and the like. Pathology was to Freud the norm; it reveals what we are really like: aggressive, hard, and full of instinctual savagery. Winnicott thinks differently:

> it is not necessary to give inborn aggression more than that which is its due in company with everything else that is inborn.
>
> (Winnicott 1982: 109)

> We tend to think of health in terms of the state of ego defences. We say it is healthy when these defences are not rigid, etc. But we seldom reach the point at which we can start to describe what life is like apart from illness or absence of illness.
>
> (p. 116)

Winnicott's answer to this lack of understanding of what life is about is that health should be sought in the nature of creativity: 'creativity [is] a feature of life and total living' (p. 64); '[it is] a colouring of the whole attitude to external reality. It is creative apperception more than anything else that makes the individual feel that life is worth living' (p. 76); 'creativity . . . belongs to being alive' (p. 79). But, 'where psychoanalysis has attempted to tackle the subject of creativity it has to a large extent lost sight of the main theme' (p. 18).

This may seem no more than a reversal of values, a matter of exchanging one set of postulates for another. And if that were the case then it would not amount to very much. Simply claiming that humans are in their nature creative instead of claiming that they are destructive is only a matter of ideology. But Winnicott's thought penetrates the problem with far greater incisiveness.

In his earlier work he had already established an independence from his Kleinian background by stressing the importance of factors that do not belong to the child's inner reality. He referred to them as the facilitating environment and he principally meant by this the role of the mother in the upbringing of the child. This was already a significant shift from the established theory which privileges the inner life over the external reality, but he still used categories which are easily accommodated within the psychoanalytical idiom, that is, he thought in terms of inside–outside. So inside there is the true and false self system – and in the true self Winnicott locates his optimism, so to speak; outside there is the environment which may or may not facilitate development. But in his last writings Winnicott develops a line of thought which runs radically against the basic principles of psychoanalysis. It is his idea of play. What makes it so original is that it is in this notion that Winnicott undoes the all-encompassing distinction between the inside and outside: 'play is in fact neither a matter of inner psychic reality nor a matter of external reality' (1982: 113); 'where are we (if anywhere at all)? We have used the concepts of inner and outer, and we want a third concept' (p. 124).

Winnicott is doing more than just adding a third dimension to the inside–outside duality. He imbues it with characteristics which are altogether different from the world of inner reality. This zone is not subject to the laws of the pleasure and reality principles.

> when a child is playing the masturbatory element is essentially lacking; or in other words, if when a child is playing the physical excitment of instinctual involvement becomes evident, then the playing stops, or is at any rate spoiled.
>
> (1982: 45)

> the phenomena that I am describing have no climax . . . these phenomena of the play area have infinite variability, contrasting with the relative stereotypy of phenomena that relate either to personal body functioning or to environmental actuality.
>
> (pp. 115, 116)

The capacity to play is the capacity to be creative, it is the capacity to change. We can change, we are creative, when we find the space of play, the space which is not governed by the laws of determinism. The space of play is not teleological. This is as radical a reversal of Freud's or Klein's determinism as one could imagine.

Such a different theoretical stance had effects on Winnicott's way of working. There too, he broke many of the established rules. He frequently arranged sessions which exceeded the prescribed fifty minutes. And Winnicott's attitude to the role of interpretation in the psychoanalytical work is most characteristic. He points out that one cannot treat all the utterances of the patient in the same way, because not everything has the same significance. Some things are important, some are not. Some may indicate deep underlying problems, some may not mean anything at all.

> [there are] unrelated thought sequences which the analyst will do well to accept as such, not assuming the existence of a significant thread . . . organized nonsense is already a defence, just as organized chaos is a denial of chaos.
>
> (1982: 65)

Winnicott argues time and again that interpretation can hinder rather than help. It is too often a way in which the therapist exercises his cleverness, or worse stunts the patient: 'interpretation outside the ripeness of the material is indoctrination and produces compliance' (p. 59).

It is necessary to be able to wait. Sometimes it is better not to interpret at all. In this way the patient may arrive at his or her own interpretation. More important than a good interpretation is that the patient develops the capacity to play.

> Psychotherapy takes place in the overlap of two areas of playing, that of the patient and that of the therapist. Psychotherapy has to do with two people playing. The corollary of this is that where playing is not possible then the work done by the therapist is directed towards bringing the patient from a state of not being able to play into a state of being able to play.
>
> (1982: 44)

And, 'If the therapist cannot play, then he is not suitable for work' (p. 63).

What emerges from these few quotations is a certain outlook in which the world appears quite different. The central element, it seems, is Winnicott's move away from the deterministic stance of psychoanalysis. This is most pronounced in the notion of creativity and play. By positing the space of play Winnicott unhinges the grip of the pleasure and reality principles. And so he thinks of therapy as a place where the patient can learn to be creative and independent rather than be indocrinated. He believes that people can be healthy and happy and that they have a right to it.

*   *   *

Winnicott's thinking presents a difficulty. On the one hand his ideas draw from the vocabulary and imagery of psychoanalysis. Such terms as projection, introjection and unconsciousness figure prominently in his writing, and as such, one can quite easily place him in a wider psychoanalytical context. Then on the other hand comes the concept of play and space of play, which cannot be accepted within the logic of psychoanalysis. Winnicott's tactic is to ask 'for a paradox to be accepted and tolerated, and for it not to be resolved' (1982: xii). But asking this of a hard-core psychoanalyst is virtually asking the impossible. Conceptualizing, explaining and resolving are needs very deeply rooted in the psychoanalytical temperament. Winnicott's notion of the space of play escapes it. One can see how the idea develops from his earlier writings on the transitional phenomena. There the distinction between the inner and outer has already become loosened. It is a most imaginative way of opening the Kleinian monad and moving from the world as projection to the world as real, and on the way Winnicott explored many important problems. But the transitional phenomena are underpinned by the notion of unconscious destructiveness which like an engine drives the process along. With this Winnicott still privileges the zone of libidinal energy.

The space of play moves one step further, or at least that is what some of what Winnicott says would suggest. It has nothing to do with the unconscious, or with the so-called external reality. It is a freak, a paradox, an inexplicable lightness which breaks up the totality of the inside–outside dialectic; 'we need a third concept'. This third concept will not be found in psychoanalysis. This is not due to a shortcoming of its conceptual matrix; it is because it is to the bone opposed to any such notion. Ideas like this sabotage its whole edifice. The difficulty that it poses has to do with notions which are central to the psycho-analytical *Weltanschauung*:[6] causality, determinism, destiny, fate.

These were at the centre of the debates in ancient Greece. Most of the Greeks were inclined to accept some degree of determinism and causation. The most extreme were the Stoics. They held that everything happens by fate and nothing springs up spontaneously. The passage of time is like the unwinding of a rope, bringing about nothing new and unrolling each stage in turn. Freud would adhere to this Stoic view. It is true, he did not like the idea of fate or predestination, but he does not remove them, he simply translates them into the language of psychical forces.

The ancient debates came to an end with the advent of the Christian doctrine. From then on causality and determinism overview human life. It is a double vice-grip: on the one hand the idea of Providence, on the other the inescapable burden of the original sin. The two, intimately linked, operate a dialectic of life and death, of being and nothingness, and within this world-view the modern version of tradition is born. This is where the Freudian discourse most properly belongs. Freud may reject the idea of Providence but he readily accepts that humans are irrevocably chained to suffering. Winnicott tellingly observes that 'the concept of the death instinct could be described as a reassertion of the principal of original sin' (1982: 82). The idea of the original sin is present in Freud from the beginning. First the crime: the sexual wish (the forbidden fruit), then punishment: castration. It should be noted that Freud does not conceive of death itself as punishment. He cannot because he quite specifically rejects any idea of God, so there is no one to dispense it. Death as punishment would also give meaning to death and this Freud does not accept.[7] But for all the differences, the Freudian project is, from a certain perspective, nothing else but a re-working of the Christian (Pauline and Augustinian, to be precise) anthropology, only without its rhetoric and without the concept of Providence.[8]

*   *   *

In the idea of play Winnicott is pointing to a very different way of thinking. He is searching for a principle which would be free from any causality; he wants to place in that principle that which gives life its worth; and the ultimate aim of life according to Winnicott seems to be well-being. This notion cannot be explored either in psychoanalysis itself or in its philosophical heritage. Winnicott's views, should one wish to seek ancient antecedents, are closer to the Epicurean position. There we find a consistent world-view which is constructed around indeterminacy. The human mind is not subject to any causality, natural or divine. The Epicurean system is based on a constant swerving away (it is known in the language of Lucretius as the *clinamen*) from fate. Being able to understand that determinism and teleology are only creations of misguided reasoning will bring peace of mind and happiness. Winnicott's closest counterpart in contemporary philosophy is Bachelard. He, too, made the stand against notions which posit a homogeneity of experience. Such discourses, he says, obviate all difference, discontinuities, and thus the possibility of anything new happening. What seems like a continuous flux is in fact broken up by what Bachelard calls moments of interregna. He refers to these moments as repose, and this seems an intuition which is almost exactly the same as Winnicott's space of play. Bachelard's writings on the poetic imagination explore that space of the interregnum, and he shows that this space is not a mere gap, just a fleeting and elusive moment; it is the principle of life, an entire universe.[9]

Thus one finds in Winnicott's writings two trends, two lines of thought. One is the psychoanalytical and most of what that entails, and the other evolves from the concept of play. The difficulty is that these two are at odds with each other. Their respective starting points are so different, one being the celebration of death, the other of being alive, that they cannot co-exist. Anyone who knows the history of philosophy knows that Epicurus enjoyed the doubtful privilege of being the most hated, by those who came later, of all the Greek philosophers.[10]

*   *   *

Psychoanalysis had its beginnings in the cathartic method. There, the psychotherapeutic process involved the diagnosis of the traumatic past event, then the patient's insight into it, and finally its abreaction. At the root of this way of thinking lies the premiss that the affect attached to the past event, even if one is not conscious of it, exerts a constant pressure and in some cases produces symptoms. The model is mechanical. The mind is supposed to operate like a machine with a circulation and distribution of energy. If the level of energy is too high, or the 'quota of affect' (Freud's own term) too charged, the machine (mind) begins to malfunction. Abreaction would then be akin to opening a valve and letting excess energy escape. In some instances this way of thinking may even seem quite useful. Symptoms are sometimes known to disappear when an earlier event, temporarily forgotten, is brought back to light. But Freud's penchant for speculative thinking could not be satisfied with such a simple view and he very early on came to reject the importance of catharsis in the psychotherapeutic process. Nevertheless, the concept of abreaction, albeit in a changed form, has never quite disappeared from Freud's work. It is also not clear whether subsequent psychotherapeutic practice has really significantly moved away from it. Such notions as transference, repetition, working through, bear its stamp. The basic elements of the abreaction thinking remain and there is an inherent danger in them.

The young man discovers that he is born to protect his father from depressive feelings. This makes a great deal understandable. His fear of death, panic attacks, obsessive thoughts about his girl-friend dying in a car accident, all these begin to make sense. But it is a grave realization which is accompanied by an array of feelings and thoughts that are not easy to handle. In a way his entire *raison d'être* is at stake. He has been handed over an existence with a strictly defined role. If he betrays his role (for example takes up his artistic leanings, though no doubt it is all more complicated) his right of existence is put into question. He may even be inclined to feel that the scenario behind his conception, that he is born to replace those who are dead, already invalidates his existence ('I might as well not have been born at all'). He will experience difficult moments.

It would seem quite natural to accept as obvious that in therapy all such feelings should be dealt with, that some process of working-through needs to take place. However, the problem is that working-through instead of dealing with the problem may foster its repetition. That which the patient wants to solve is constantly re-enacted in therapy, and the patient may finish imprisoned in the past. He comes to therapy because he feels locked in a causal circle. His sense of identity is centred on that past. He feels that his future is already pre-determined by it. That is who he senses he is and he cannot give it away. So he will force the therapist to spend a great deal of time on 'working through the problem'. That is an inherent need for the patient. But it has nothing to do with abreaction, he simply needs to begin to see his past. This is crucial. Without this it is difficult to see how he could attempt to free himself from it. The power of the past lies in its hiddenness. If one is kept in the dark one will feel haunted by some malignant fate. What would Oedipus' life be if he knew from the outset that the names of his real parents were Laius and Jocasta; that he was born into a curse because his father as a young man had raped his best friend's son; that his parents wanted to have him killed soon after he was born? This is a futile question, one cannot even begin to try to answer it. But it makes one think. One wonders if Oedipus would have been so irrevocably fated if he knew all this. For there to be a tragedy as we know it, it is essential that all that precedes Oedipus is hidden from him. Yet it is one thing to know the past and another to be free from it. One may know all and still feel helpless in the face of it. Feeling driven mad is not just an effect of what has once happened in the past but the fact that for one reason or another one feels that it is impossible to get out, that all options are closed off. This often gives that strange affliction which is called ennui. It is the odium that comes from being perpetually enclosed, of being condemned by the past, without anything other ever appearing in sight. Such a feeling often leads people to seek psychotherapy.

The past is not a uniform concept. It may concern that which happened before one was born, as in the case of the young man who wanted to be an artist, as well as events from the actual lived past. Yet in some respects the issue is always similar: the past closes off the future and a change in attitude to the past is essential. A simple and revealing illustration of just such a problem comes from a workshop of R. D. Laing.[11] A young woman is relating to him a problem that is haunting her. When she was 6 or 7 she was abused sexually by her father. But what she cannot remember is whether her father had intercourse with her or not. Sometimes she thinks he only sexually played with her, sometimes she thinks that he went all the way. The memory is too elusive, and however much she tries to remember the incident she does not succeed in making it any clearer. She is stuck with not being able to remember. That is her problem. Laing answers, 'Your future does not depend on that', and he goes on to tell her that only if she realizes that, only then, will she be free to remember the incident rather than be haunted by it. In this one dense comment Laing opens up something new for the woman. He is telling her that her life need not be governed by the childhood event, and so he is aiming to break one of her most fundamental convictions. That may be the most important thing that any therapist has ever told her. But there is more to it. Laing is not telling her to forget the incident, nothing of the sort. He is telling her that she cannot remember because of the importance that she attaches to it. To put it differently, she represses because she is locked in a causal system of self-reference. If she could give up the belief that the incident has to determine the shape of her life she would be free to remember.

The example from Laing's workshop does not resolve the problem of the hiddenness of the past; it in fact refers to something quite different, the vagueness of memory. Nevertheless, Laing's dictum, 'Your future does not depend on your past', should be taken seriously as the first step in reshaping one's attitude to anything that concerns the past. Furthermore this line of reasoning leads to the following thought: the idea of repression has its roots in the concept of causality. Linking events into an unbreakable chain of cause and effect closes the possibility of anything new happening. If everything that has happened in the past determines the future then the only way to create a space which would give the semblance of freedom, however illusory, is to forget. And when both the patient and the therapist share this point of view then all the working-through, interpreting, etc., may just become a vicious circle.

The chain of cause and effect is not a given fact. Even if it feels that way to the patient, it certainly is not all there is, and it is not as tightly woven as some would have it. The future does not depend on the past as though it was some law of physics. Realizing this may be a condition for the appearance of Winnicott's space of play.

*   *   *

For a long time it was thought that the universe follows well-rounded laws. Observation seemed to confirm that most phenomena behave according to them. That made sense, this is how reason or God would no doubt have it. When physicists noticed that some phenomena have certain irregularities (such as the not so regular movement of the pendulum, for example) they also discovered that, so as not to disturb this orderly universe, Newtonian mechanics was actively marginalizing and flattening out these oddities. When the scientists focused more of their attention on these irregularities they formulated the theory of relativity and quantum physics, and things never looked the same again. Something of the sort is needed in the field of psychotherapy. Clearly, it is not the case of 'applying' the new schema of physics to the practice of psychotherapy; the rules of one game are not suitable for another. Yet the monochrome repetitiveness of the psychoanalytical process is punctuated by odd utterances, unusual moods, by all sorts of moments that are out of place. Freud himself came across such oddities early on but as they did not suit his way of thinking he pushed them to the margins. One such oddity appears at a significant moment, which concerns the cornerstone of the doctrine, the theory of memory and forgetfulness. Freud encountered memories which seemed very clear and at the same time utterly banal. But he operated with a single mechanism of forgetting and recollection which at first could not account for these clear and (to Freud) meaningless memories. Freud resolved to name them 'screen memories' and he argued that their unusual clarity is due to a ruse of the unconscious which uses such innocent memories to conceal behind them repressed sexual experiences or fantasies. These memories, just like slips of the tongue and other parapraxes, are essentially symptoms.

But there is more to forgetting and recollecting than that. There is indeed a heavy memory which weaves a thread of injury and suffering, hard and unchanging, and this is what we have been taught to call identity. This is subject to repression. But there is also memory which is light, where courage and inventiveness take root, and in which new exploits and ventures begin. These memories are not repressed but simply forgotten. They do get recounted in the psychoanalytical sessions, as are also other unusual instances. Yet all too often, because they are unusual, they remain on an anecdotal level. It is a matter of thinking about these deviations from the psychoanalytical norm, not as exceptions, but systematically. This is the point where Winnicott's ideas are so useful. The 'third term' between the inner and the outer is an opening where a different horizon appears, where the forces of instinct and reality can be laid to rest. One need not necessarily follow all of Winnicott's reasoning, one may quibble at the ample usage of psychoanalytical terminology and imagery, but at least what he says has the merit of being thoroughly thought through. Winnicott did not proceed from a neat concept to which he later fitted observations and speculations. Quite the contrary, he arrived at the notion of play slowly via the idea of transitional phenomena, and after finding it he then struggled to formulate it without having a ready-made language at his disposal. That space of play is a deviation from the psycho-analytical norm, and, as it clearly emerges from Winnicott's utterances, in this deviation lies the principle of healing. The other great merit of Winnicott's thinking is not only that it undoes the tightness of the psychoanalytical theorizing but that it also questions its practice, that it makes demands on the therapist: 'If the therapist cannot play, then he is not suitable for the work.'

The concept of playing looks simple. But this is deceptive because it has two precepts which are far from easy to follow. First, one must not think of it in terms of the inner and outer, and second, it is neither causal nor teleological. It would thus seem aimless and ephemeral and yet it is at the heart of the capacity to be creative and to change. Thinking about this space of play invites scepticism in relation to psychoanalytical theories, to any ready-made theory.[12] It will make one look for the unusual rather than repetition. It will make the therapist far more alert and, just as Winnicott exhorts, prepared to accept paradox without explaining it away. Our carefully constructed logic and heavy-footed dialectics are good at explaining illness but when it comes to creativity and well-being they let us down. Well-being escapes conceptualization. One may be alert to it but one cannot put it in a fixed framework. It takes a particular vigilance to be on the look-out for well-being in patients without lapsing into a sentimentalism. Moreover, one cannot accept one of the earlier ideas of Winnicott (followed later by Laing) about an established 'true self' lurking behind, waiting to come out into the open and blossom. That is wishful thinking, and the patients probably know that best. And because they know it so well the therapist will encounter strong resistance. There is an attachment to illness – Freud already noted it – which gives a sense of identity, and which will not go away. It seems that the misery of the enclosure of illness is more tolerable than the anxiety that is provoked by what may wait outside (and there may be nothing). Every psychotherapist knows that some patients end up using therapy to perpetuate their malaise. But that is the part of the story which is governed by repetition, the other part, less conspicuous, is made up of all the deviations.

These little swervings could be the beginnings of new narratives. What is at stake is a need to develop a phenomenology of illness and well-being in which repetition, causality and teleology have no place. There is not much to start off with: a few scraps, an odd screen memory; it can be anything that does not somehow fit. It should be about privileging the exception and turning it into a norm. One could start by thinking up collages, helping the patients to re-create their own mythologies. There may be resistance, but it is also just as much the question of habit, so it takes time. But if one is at it for long enough, and with persistence, these seemingly meagre beginnings may become richer, and perhaps Bachelard's idea of a 'poetic destiny' would even begin to make sense.[13]

One cannot deny that there is something which is referred to as history; that there is custom, habit, heritage, ancestry, legacy, lineage. People have memories, and they also forget. There are also events which, as they say, 'change the course of life', which are unforgettable, even if at the same time repressed. All this, one way or another, 'is' behind. This much is uncontestable. The question is how it is behind, whether this past exists in such a fashion that it can claim someone as its possession. If it appears to threaten to do so, then it is necessary to be able to announce a unilateral declaration of independence. Otherwise, one will be condemned to repetition and unable to create, life will seem mapped out in advance, and one will end up accepting suffering as one's just lot. This message of independence should be a *sine qua non* for the patient. If the therapist does not facilitate this attitude and instead, in the name of his tradition, indoctrinates the patient then we witness not healing but violence.

POSTSCRIPT

While ruminating on tradition and its place in psychotherapy a nagging thought kept recurring to me. It first came up in a form of a question: If Freud's concept of the death drive was a reaction to the events of the First World War (that is one way of looking at it), then how would he have responded to the Holocaust? Genocide is not new in the history of humanity but this time it seems different. It happened here, not in some far-away African or Asian land, but here in the heart of our civilization. It has penetrated that most European of inventions: *Geist*, it has become part of the (un)conscious with which the psychoanalyst deals.

Would Freud then go on and develop his unconscious, now filling it up with something like Canetti's 'heap of the dead'?[14] Or would he just grind his teeth and mutter, 'Didn't I say so all along?' It is hard to tell. And what has this got to do with tradition? This is what makes the nagging thought keep recurring. Lacan says that the horror of Nazism cannot be explained on Hegelian–Marxist premises (whatever that really means), and he invokes the idea of the 'dark god' (Lacan 1979: 275). It probably cannot be explained on any premises. Maybe this is because it has always been there, at the very heart of the dialectic of tradition; in the stench of the Inquisition; in those images of burning sinners that the early apologists took pleasure in showing; or perhaps already in Plato's cave. Maybe that continuous parricide of which Freud spoke produced such a heap of the dead that it finally exploded and spilled over. It cannot be explained, but it happened, and it is here to stay. The survivors of the Holocaust often found it impossible to speak about the experience. Some wrote about it, and some of those who tried to face it squarely ended in committing suicide. Now psychotherapists are seeing the children of the survivors of the Holocaust, they are dealing with a very particular hand-over. And what they are coming up against is something which is difficult to grasp, an experience which is beyond the endurable, non-integratable, non-assimilible, non-justifiable, something which cannot be synthesized within any synthesis. It is pure excess.[15] Always beyond but sucking in like a black hole.

Why bring this up? What is the place in it for such ideas as 'space of play', or 'poetic destiny'? It needs to be brought up because tradition has a murky lining and psychotherapy is an ethical enterprise which concerns itself with such matters; because psychotherapy is in the business of remembering, not forgetting; and because more and more patients bring this with them into the consulting rooms. Ideas like 'poetic destiny' are not simple, they are not just lying around ready to be picked up. They have to be sought out. Notions about 'evil human nature', or 'dark god', are easy, one could even say, lazy. Such ideas lead nowhere. Or, to quote a memorable line from Artaud, 'It is the question of knowing what we want. If we are all prepared for war, plague, famine, and slaughter, we do not even need to say so, we have only to go on as we are' (Artaud 1988: 255). But then, T. S. Eliot reminds us that what is to come still awaits another voice.[16]

NOTES

1 Although Freud's revelation to Fleiss is also the first formulation of the Oedipus complex it was the more general theory of childhood sexuality which marked out psychoanalysis in its early years. The full Oedipus complex is only worked out about a decade later.

2 Masud Khan, for example, begins the Editorial Preface to *The Language of Psychoanalysis* with the following: 'Since Socrates, in European cultures one would be hard put to find a thinker and scientist more humble, more self-questioning and more self-convinced than Sigmund Freud' (Laplanche and Pontalis 1980: v).

3 This, in main, is the thesis that Francois Roustang puts forward (Roustang 1892). The striking feature of the book is that after scanning the issues of discipleship in psychoanalysis he ends with a chapter where he formulates a theory of psychosis and which draws its main insight from the analysis of this discipleship.

4 The *kherem* under which Spinoza was placed would be one such example.

5 The context is the family origin. This is not to say that it is necessarily the sole, or even most important, reason that someone becomes a patient. Yet it is also true that virtually every psychotherapy will at some stage deal with the issue of family.

6 One cannot accept the claim of Freud, and of Lacan after him, that psychoanalysis does not have a *Weltanschauung*.

7 The closing paragraphs of *The Ego and the Id*, in which Freud argues against the significance of death and that the fear of death is a development of the fear of castration, are quite relevant here (Freud 1923: 58–9).

8 A detailed study would show how much Freud remains within Augustine's anthropology. One similarity is in this context particularly significant. A bitter doctrinal dispute in which Augustine was embroiled was over whether infants are born sinful. Augustine's opponent, Pelagius, argued against this, whereas Augustine was of the view that infants are born with

the mark of sin, and that is why the new-born has to be baptised immediately. Augustine won the argument and the whole matter became Church doctrine. It is exactly this notion, that children are born as 'polymorphous perverts', that Breuer could not go along with, although he was perfectly open to linking problems of sexuality and neurosis. It was this non-acceptance of the idea of childhood sexuality (i.e. perversity) that made him in the eyes of Freud a heretic and traitor.

9   All Bachelard writings on the poetic imagination, that is, the books on water, air, and earth, *Poetics of Space*, *Poetics of Reverie*, are relevant here.

10 Not until the seventeenth-century commentary of Gassendi was there anything but vilification of all Epicurean thought.

11 This comes in a film made in 1989 by Third Mind Productions Inc., Vancouver, Canada, *Did You Used to Be R. D. Laing?*, which was shown on Channel 4 a few months after Laing's death.

12 Scepticism of the psychoanalytical theory is always implicit in Winnicott's work. A more explicit sceptical stance comes in the late writings of another eminent psychoanalyst from the Kleinian stable, Wilfred Bion.

13 Bachelard asks, 'Would it not then be that poetry is not an accident, a detail, a diversion of being? Might poetry be the very principle of creative evolution? Will man have a poetic destiny?' (Bachelard 1950: xi).

14 Canetti does not follow Freud's thinking. He is in fact singularly hostile to the idea of the unconscious. And yet, *Crowds and Power* reads like an addendum to Freud. The book ends with an interpretation of the case of Judge Schreber which is very different from that of Freud's. Interestingly, Canetti thinks that Freud could not have given a better interpretation because it dates from before the horrors of the two world wars.

15 It is in these terms that Levinas writes about evil (Levinas 1987: 180).

16 The exact words are two lines in *Little Gidding* (lines 7 and 8, p. 218, in the *Collected Poems*, 1909–1962, Faber & Faber, 1974).

REFERENCES

Artaud, A. (1988) 'The theatre and its double', in Antonian Artaud, *Selected Writings*, Los Angeles: University of California Press.

Bachelard, G. (1950) *La dialectique de la durée*, Paris: Presses Universitaires de France.

Canetti, E. (1981) *Crowds and Power*, Harmondsworth: Penguin Books.

Ellenberger, H. (1970) *The Discovery of the Unconscious*, New York: Basic Books.

Freud, S. (1892) *Standard Edition of the Complete Psychological Works of Sigmund Freud*, 24 vols, 1953–74, edited by J. Strachey, London: Hogarth Press (SE) 1.

——— (1950 [1892–1899]) 'Extracts from the Fliess Papers', SE 1.

——— (1895) with Breuer, J. *Studies on Hysteria*, SE 2.

——— (1899) 'Screen memories', in SE 3.

——— (1910) 'Five lectures on psycho-analysis', in SE 11.

——— (1914) 'On the history of the psycho-analytic movement', in SE 14.

——— (1920) *Beyond the Pleasure Principle*, SE 18.

Lacan, J. (1979) *The Four Fundamental Concepts of Psycho-Analysis*, Harmondsworth: Penguin Books.

Laplanche, J. and Pontalis, J.-B. (1980) *The Language of Psychoanalysis*, London: Hogarth Press.

Levinas, E. (1987) 'Transcendence and evil', in Emmanuel Levinas, *Collected Philosophical Papers*, Dordrecht: Nijhoff.

Roustang, F. (1982) *Dire Mastery*, Baltimore, Md.: Johns Hopkins University Press.

Winnicott, D. W. (1982) *Playing and Reality*, Harmondsworth: Penguin Books.

Name index

Aberbach, David 41
Abraham, H. C. 44
Adler, Alfred 138
Aenesidemus 119
Alexander the Great 118
Anaxarchus 118
Andersen, Hans 3–4
Anna, O. 138–40
Annas, Julia 119
Anzieu, Didier 116
Apollo 57, 108
Aron, W. 47n
Artaud, Antonin 155
Asclepius 50, 57–9, 73, 108
Augustine 116, 155n

Bachelard, Gaston 148, 153, 156n
Barham, Peter 35
Barker, M. 30
Barnes, Jonathan 119
Barthes, Roland 130
Berenson, Bernhard 80, 82
Bergmann, M. S. 47n
Berkower, L. 47n
Bernays, Emmeline 42
Bertram, G. 58
Bion, Wilfred 12, 15–16, 62, 125, 156n
Blatt, D. S. 47n
Bloom, Harold 7
Bollas, Christopher 80
Breuer, Josef 44, 137–40
Burke, Edmund 96

Canetti, Elias 130, 154, 156n

Cavell, Stanley 123
Celsus 120
Chiron 57, 108
Clancier, Anne 93–4
Coronis 57
Cuddihy, J. M. 47n

Dante Alighieri 35
Darwin, Charles 35, 111
David, King 8
Descartes, René 119, 128–9
Dickens, Charles 35
Diogenes Laertius 119
Dourley, J. P. 73
Duncan, Mark 122
Durkheim, Émile 46

Edinger, E. F. 73
Einstein, Albert 35
Eliade, Mircea 49, 55–7, 69, 71
Eliot, T. S. 3, 89–90, 95, 155
Ellenberger, Henri 139
Epicurus 148
Erasmus 49, 119
Erikson, Erik 11
Estienne, Henri 119
Evans, Richard 51

Fairbairn, Ronald 92
Falk, A. 47n
Ferenczi, Sandor 97, 115
Finney, Brian 26, 28, 36–7
Fliess, Wilhelm 135
Fogelin, R. J. 129
Fordham, Michael 70, 71

Subject index

For Product Safety Concerns and Information please contact our EU
representative GPSR@taylorandfrancis.com
Taylor & Francis Verlag GmbH, Kaufingerstraße 24, 80331 München, Germany